The
Southern Way

The regular volume for the Southern devotee

Kevin Robertson

Issue 51

ISBN 9781909328983

First published in 2020 by Noodle Books
an imprint of Crécy Publishing Ltd

New contact details
All editorial submissions to:
The Southern Way (Kevin Robertson)
'Silmaril'
Upper Lambourn
Hungerford
Berkshire RG17 8QR
Tel: 01488 674143
editorial@thesouthernway.co.uk

Publisher's note: Every effort has been made to
identify and correctly attribute photographic
credits. Any error that may have occurred is
entirely unintentional.

Printed in the UK by Short Run Press

Noodle Books is an imprint of
Crécy Publishing Limited
1a Ringway Trading Estate
Shadowmoss Road
Manchester M22 5LH

www.crecy.co.uk

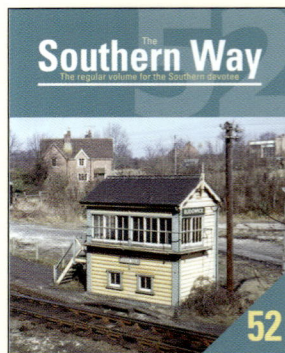

Issue No 52 of THE SOUTHERN WAY
ISBN 9781909328990
available in October 2020 at £14.95
To receive your copy the moment it is
released, order in advance from your usual
supplier, or it can be sent post-free (UK)
direct from the publisher:

Crécy Publishing Ltd (Noodle Books)

1a Ringway Trading Estate, Shadowmoss
Road, Manchester M22 5LH

Tel 0161 499 0024

www.crecy.co.uk

enquiries@crecy.co.uk

Front cover:
**Memories of summer times…a bracing crossing of the
Solent with a train journey from Ryde to Sandown,
Shanklin or Ventnor; perhaps if you were lucky, a
beautifully clean engine as well. No 22 *Brading,* fresh
from overhaul at Ryde St Johns, and a slightly more
work stained No 32 *Bonchurch* behind.**
Peter Gray/Great Western Trust

Rear cover:
**Almost in the camp of the opposition, 'U' class 2-6-0
No 31635 stands outside Reading (Southern shed); the
WR main line runs east-west on a slightly higher level.
The old adage from (G)WR days also seems to apply, '…
if in doubt – add a signal..!'** *J Barnsey*

Title page:
**Notwithstanding the headcode, we suspect somewhere in
the West Country and probably west of Exeter. Traction is
'N' Class Mogul No 31846 with a mixed freight, including,
up front, a couple of milk tanks**. *J Barnsey*

Contents

Introduction

I don't know if you are like me whenever I travel by train nowadays, but I tend to find myself constantly thinking back into history, seemingly with each mile that passes. 'That used to be the junction for...', or 'So and so signal box and sidings were once there...', nostalgia, or a desire to live in the past without embracing the present? My wife would probably say the latter but I would sincerely hope the former, although still being prepared to move part-way with the times.

With the inability of science to come up with a ready time machine enabling me to go back, shake Mr Bulleid by the hand and simply ask him 'why'?, I must instead content myself with drawing upon the research and recollections of others in order to further my seemingly insatiable quest for ever more railway knowledge. Why is it also that whilst walking the dog one afternoon I was able to recite all the 'Merchant Navy' names and most of those from the 'West Country' class (I always did get mixed up with the 'Squadrons') and yet ask me to recall the name of an actor seen on TV just a couple of days before and the mind goes blank.

Fifty issues back (actually 51 of course), I was expounding on the concept of 'SW' and what you might expect to see. Well, for the start of the second half-century I can only repeat what I mentioned in No 50 that, unless I am instructed otherwise (by you), we will continue as before. I can say that I do receive emails with requests for items to appear but whether that is possible depends very much on what has arrived to be included or who I might 'prod' to undertake the work.

Meanwhile I can tell you I have personally been busy and, with the new Crécy catalogue for the summer and early autumn released, I am delighted to announce that the 'Special' issue for the autumn of this year will be on the Southern oil-burning engines in the period 1946-51. Indeed, what had started off with the intention of being a simple article, grew and grew with the result that 40,000 words of text, 10,000 words of captions and 104 images later I think we are finished. BUT – there are still some gaps, notably concerning images of the fixed installations at Fratton, Eastleigh and Exmouth Junction. Also of the 'cuckoo in the nest', ie the converted No 34036 *Westward Ho* working a train in oil burning condition. Why call it a 'cuckoo', well there is a very valid reason but you will have to wait for the autumn to find out. But if you can help with anything on the subject, I would be most grateful.

I mention the period '1946-51' as being the timescale that I am covering and I can almost hear you say, '...hey, how about 1925...' and so on. Simply put, there was no room but I can promise that the earlier oil burners will be dealt with as a stand-alone article in *SW52* which will appear in October.

As before, thank you for all your support and I sincerely hope you enjoy what we have on offer in the pages that follow.

Finally, we are sad to report the passing of another long term Southern enthusiast, J H (Jim) Aston in January. Jim was active as a photographer, certainly from the late 1940s onwards, and also produced superb quality prints on double-weight gloss paper. We have used several in our publications over the years and when asked for a print of a particular subject and gaining a positive response, you knew it would be of excellent quality.

Writing these last few lines in May 2020, I can look out on what is a wonderful late spring day, grass and flowers gently bending in the breeze and all is right with the world. But of course in truth we know the opposite. The devastation caused by the pandemic has affected every one of us. At best a restriction on movement, at worst – well the statistics tell us that.

Like the rest of the Crécy team I am working from home. We have telephone and 'Zoom' type meetings (I wonder what Messrs Walker and Bulleid would have made of such things – I suspect thoroughly approved) whilst many of you have been so kind in not just sending congratulatory notes on reaching No 50, but also with material and ideas for future content. Thank you all.

However, we also have to be realistic. No outdoor events, no book shops, and no heritage railways (at the time of writing) mean *SW* may be more difficult to locate. Please therefore use our subscription and mail order services – or support your usual retailer in the same way. If you are reading this then it means No 51 has been released, I promise No 52 will also be well on the way to completion and we have plans for 53 and beyond. Be assured I am certainly NOT using the lockdown as any form of excuse to stop, we will continue into the future.

But it does also mean there *may* be some delays to some future publication dates – or there may not be. Hopefully this issue will have appeared in July and similarly, hopefully, No 52 and Special 17 (specifically referred to in the final article within this issue) in October.

Perhaps by that time we will have returned to normal – whatever normal is by then. We may be prevented from following our hobbies and interests out of doors but be assured indoors there is still plenty to report upon and describe.

Kevin Robertson

Field Trip to Crystal Palace

Alan Postlethwaite

Somewhere we have not visited for a little time is Bournemouth West. Standing at Platform 5 is 'M7' Class 0-4-4T No 30254, soon to depart for Brockenhurst via Poole, Broadstone, Wimborne and Ringwood, the 'old road' as it was referred to and with a journey time in the order of 70 minutes for the thirty miles including ten intermediate stops. Built in 1897 the engine had a life of 67 years until withdrawn together with the remaining members of the class in 1964. *J Barnsey*

The LB&SCR's Crystal Palace Low Level station opened in 1854, the terminus of a short branch from the Brighton main line at Sydenham. It became a through station with extensions to London Victoria (1856), Norwood Junction (1857) and Beckenham Junction (1858). It carried all the London, Chatham and Dover Railway (LC&DR) traffic to Victoria until the Chatham's Metropolitan Extension opened in 1863. The Low Level station was rebuilt in 1875 in a lavish French or Italian style with a clerestory roof over the booking hall and a carriage canopy (*porte cochère*) with ornate ironwork. Triumphal stone staircases led to the platforms below. No expense was spared. The station offered easy access to Crystal Palace gardens but it was a long trudge up the hill to the pavilions of the Great Exhibition. In that respect, the LC&DR had the edge. I discovered the Low Level station a year after my field trip to walk the LC&DR line to the High Level terminus. *Alan Postlethwaite, 1959. All photographs are copyright of the Bluebell Railway Photographic Archives*

The branch to Crystal Palace High Level opened in 1865 with intermediate stations at Peckham Rye, Nunhead, Honor Oak, Lordship Lane and Upper Sydenham. The line was electrified in 1925 but traffic dwindled, especially after destruction of the Palace by fire in 1936, leading to closure of the branch south of Nunhead in 1954. Here, a 4-SUB unit to Crystal Palace arrives at Lordship Lane. Like Honor Oak, the station had wooden platforms and no goods yard. Note the lamp posts painted with white stripes for the wartime blackout. Shortly after moving with my parents to East Dulwich in early 1958, my first field trip was to walk the closed line from here to the Palace. *John J Smith, 1954*

In September 1954, a special train was run to mark the closure of the High Level branch and a hundred years of rail services to Crystal Palace, the Low Level station having opened in 1854. Double headed by SE&CR class 'C' 0-6-0 Nos 31576 and 31719, the 'Palace Centenarian' ran via Peckham Rye to Clapham Junction, then round the Twickenham loop, returning to reverse at Factory Junction, then to Crystal Palace Low Level, London Bridge, Blackfriars and back to the High Level station. In this view, the empty stock is just north of Lordship Lane station. *Colin Hogg, 1954*

South of Lordship Lane station, this unusual wooden truss footbridge is set upon stone plinths. The branch had a rural character throughout, passing through much woodland. These trees are relatively young. Most of the ancient oaks had been felled to build RN warships and East Indiamen at Deptford. The New Cross turnpike had to be closed in winter due to excessive rutting caused by the horse-drawn lumber traffic. At one time, there must have been foxes hereabouts for the kennels of the former West Kent Hunt were nearby at the appropriately named Dog Kennel Hill. *Alan Postlethwaite, 1959*

These trees at Upper Sydenham are in full leaf. A few houses are visible beyond. A wooden footbridge at the far end leads to the booking office and exit on the hill. The platforms are tarmac-gravel with concrete edging and have been extended at this end. *John J Smith, 1954*

Built on a steep hillside, Upper Sydenham station building had two storeys at the front and three at the back. The booking office was integral with the station house. Before arrival of the Crystal Palace in 1854, Sydenham Hill was famous for its well. A spa was developed for the taking not only of water but of alcohol, acquiring a bad reputation. Wells Park Road looks peaceful and deserted in this 1954 scene. *John J Smith*

Upper Sydenham station building stands above Crescent Wood tunnel which took the line northwards. Its profile is more elliptical than the Paxton tunnel to Crystal Palace. Three and a half years after closure, the portal is already half-hidden by undergrowth. *Alan Postlethwaite, 1958*

I walked the Paxton tunnel to Crystal Palace. Debris adorned the buttresses that supported the ridge roadway known as Crystal Palace Parade. In the early 1950s, seven bus routes terminated on the Parade including old bus types D, Tunnel STL and single deck LT. *Alan Postlethwaite, 1959*

The High Level station was a Victorian masterpiece with one message – Grandeur. Not to be outclassed by the Brighton's Low Level station, this LC&DR portal has an elaborate blend of stone and brickwork. The white rectangle was a signal sighting shield. *Alan Postlethwaite, 1959*

To build the High Level station, major engineering work was needed to cut this flat expanse out of the hillside. One line (second up, left) led to the headshunt of a modest goods yard (mainly coal) and the steam stock sidings. In the early days of 3+2+3 formations, a 3-SUB unit plus 2-car trailer might be stored, off-peak, on each of two EMU sidings on the far right. The far mansion has a wonderful outlook. *John J Smith, 1954*

The High Level station had six wooden platform faces serving four terminal lines. The turntable was at the far end beyond the road bridge and exit to the town. Behind the camera was the Exhibition footbridge with an exotic subway leading directly to the Crystal pavilions. *Colin Hogg, 1954*

John Gaywood Click
'Engineering the Southern' Part 3

Well we did promise you some amusing – and at times serious – times from John with his stories on No 36001, and we sincerely hope you enjoy them. Before starting however, special thanks to Roderick Cameron and Stephen Duffell, both of whom have corrected me and filled in some more detail on the man himself. John was born on 24 April 1926 taking the middle name 'Gaywood', his Mother's maiden name (not as previously stated 'Gayward'). He passed away on 1 November 1988. With thanks to both (and Ancestry.com!).

The 'Leader's First Steaming

As the 'Leader' neared completion, the painters swarmed all over it, painting it black – after all, this one really was a mixed traffic locomotive. When done end to end, OVB must have come down to have a look for before the paint was properly dry, they set to once again, doing the whole of the upper works a light battleship grey look, à la GNR No 990. *(At this stage JGC was unaware that an order had come down from Marylebone stating that the engine needed to prove itself on test before being painted in its formal black livery. Hence the reversion to 'photographic grey'. For an image of the engine in black livery the reader is referred to page 37 of "The 'Leader' Project" by KJR.)*

There were irritating last minute problems but the Works 'Terrier' 377S came in and stood, panting patiently most of the morning, waiting to pull No 36001 out. At last its services were needed and, snatching on a loose coupling (an old trick), succeeded in moving its heavy load halfway out, where it promptly stuck fast. Whether it was lack of power, the tight curve, bad rail joints or (perish the thought) a design problem – or ALL *(the capitalisation is JGC's)* those things – wasn't clear; but there was only one way to go – back inside. *(It turned out Brighton Works had never had such a long vehicle inside and No 36001 had jammed against the timber framing of the exit doors. KJR.)*

> With No 36001 ensconced inside overnight, next morning it was decreed by the Chief himself that lighting up would be done in the Erecting Shop, a very unpopular move not made since No 2039's first tests. With the help of a compressed air line feeding the blower ring, steam was made surprisingly quickly without completely filling the place with smoke; though it was said that the overhead crane-man did ask for fog men to be posted on the crane rails!

Nobody, and it was very wise, really liked the idea of driving No 36001 out under its own power; so, after the track outside the door had had a facelift, an 'E4' tank, which had been specially laid on, tried its luck.

A view, which has arrived since publication of the earlier article in this series, is this one of 'Merchant Navy' No 21C4 *Cunard White Star* in charge of 15 vehicles somewhere west of Salisbury in WW2. Trains of this length – and even longer – were commonplace during WW2 but were not popular with the operators at Waterloo, as they could effectively 'lock-up' the station by standing on several track circuits simultaneously.

One slip, and...success? After about an engine length there was a loud bang, a general shout of 'WHOA', and the strongest suggestion that some foul inside or underneath had cleared itself. Something must have broken, but what? Short of taking many covers off, the cause would remain a mystery, for the present at least. No 1 bogie frame appeared to me to be hard against the main frame, and the [as above] foul could have been there; but at the next attempt out came the 'Leader', reluctant no longer. There was some protest from the flanges and an impression that the track might burst, but she was safely deposited on the Works siding adjacent to the line from Lewes.

I wanted to be there for the first move; but, calculating that I'd be missed, went back to the Drawing Office for a bit. After nearly an hour I slipped out again and they had the boiler blowing off. The Works Manager, L J Granshaw, was in No 1 cab (the chimney end) preparing to move, watched by a large number of erecting shop staff anxious not to miss the fun. Others, like me, who had no business to be there, stood back a bit trying to look at ease and hoping nobody would notice them.

Very significantly, not a soul from the design staff was there or had been invited. Had I been known to the Works Manager as one of Cocks's (the Chief Draughtsman) outfit, he would have gone out of his way to have ordered me off 'a bit sharpish'. Granshaw had a lot of testing experience behind him but it was absurd that at least Cocks wasn't there too, after all it was he who knew what everything was supposed to do. Perhaps they knew each other's limitations so well that they dared not meet and risk a very public scene.

I hoped OVB would appear, and decided to stand my ground if he did.

At about half past two Granshaw tried the whistle, from which issued water, then steam, but only a wet squeak. Instead he shouted a warning, then tugging at the regulator, watched the steam chest pressure gauge and then the ground, anticipating movement. Nothing at all happened.

The Foreman helpfully hinted that the cylinder cocks ought to be opened. This lever wanted a lot of pulling; but water, stutteringly at first, became a series of ever more powerful jets shooting out from both ends, horizontally now and flashing into steam. The unwary, who had not realised that what came out at one end would also come out at the other, moved smartly to safer ground. Hot live steam was at last issuing forth.

Chapelon's principles of having large steam pipes and big steam-chest volume in relation to cylinder size were all very well in theory but what an awful lot of water to be evacuated, how great a risk of hydraulic damage, and what would happen in freezing conditions? At least the Drawing Office had had the foresight to put a drain cock at the lowest point in each main steam pipe, though it was not an automatic one.

But why hadn't the beast moved: even shot off? Well, she was still in mid-gear but at least something had been gained; the cylinders were now pretty hot. Mr G next found the reversing lever; opting NOT to go seawards towards the buffers protecting the dangerously close main signal box, pulled it towards him. Nothing happened again.

Plainly friction in the complicated system of levers, gears and splined shafts was too much for the steam reverser. Strong men with pinch bars were next called for and they inserted these in the forked ends of the shafts going, bogie-wards, in either direction. Two and then four strong men pulled mightily without the slightest effect. Not being able to stick this any longer I ventured to suggest that the two men at one end needed to pull DOWN whilst those at the other needed to push UP. *(As 'Leader' had a power bogie at either end, each had to be 'reversed' to the same amount – or to be more accurate, one had to be in forward gear-the other reverse AND each to the same amount.)* This done, there was an immediate clonk as both bogies went into full gear, depositing two men on the ground and giving the other pair an 'uplifting' experience.

Another try was made but by now with steam shrieking from both ends, it was obvious that 36001 wanted to move, but it just didn't.

A bystander, from Accounts I think, asked very politely if, "...those wooden things with handles on..." were possibly part of the problem? Whilst these four scotches were being knocked out from either side of a wheel on each bogie, nobody had noticed the fireman 'putting a bit on'. He was not going to be caught out. I never did like 'pop' safety valves, especially with 280psi behind them, and certainly didn't now. Everyone present was startled and jumped visibly when one lifted thunderously; nerves were becoming decidedly ragged.

Someone else hazarded that the handbrake was perhaps still on. "Take the handbrake off!" shouted Mr G, adding helpfully "...it's in the fireman's cab". The fireman found the handle and did the necessary; so could anything now prevent movement? Well only if someone had thoughtfully put scotches in on the other side...they had!

I was suddenly glad that Bulleid was not there, because what had started as ardent endeavour had become knockabout farce. Whatever next?

Up to now the power brake had not been considered at all; so that, had 36001 moved off, only the handbrake or, hopefully, reverse steam in her teeth could have stopped her bounding off the 200 yards or so to the old copper shop buffers. Suppose she had demolished them and the shop walls? Farfetched? Not really: and beyond was a drop into the road far below.

Bulleid was very hot on brakes and, not at all deterred by the many novelties already aboard the 'Leader', had required Gresham and Craven's Augmented Vacuum Brake to be fitted. This was, very belatedly, now brought into use. The ejector, by the smokebox, was not under the driver's control; but, once the steam valve on the manifold down the corridor had been opened, it charged the system and then cut in and out to maintain a high vacuum in the storage cylinders. A proportioning valve ensured normal train pipe and brake cylinder topside vacuum; and the whole system, besides giving quicker brake release, avoided steam pipes in either cab; two simple horizontal banjo-type brake valves being fitted. A disadvantage was that the ejector made a loud and harsh noise up the chimney, seemingly 'going off' unpredictably, and certainly when least expected. There was only a hint, though, of the raspberry-like sound made by some GWR ejectors, originally supplied by the same manufacturer.

By the time the brakes had been tested, and found to work virtually first time, it was late afternoon. Sensibly it was decided to try again next day; for if nothing else, some of the things not to do had been found out the hard way and some time taken to ponder the afternoon's events was very desirable.

It was easy without any responsibility and not much experience to be critical and to see the funny side of it all; simpler still to write it all up after all these years; but history was to have a very strange way of repeating itself. How could I possibly have imagined then that I would find myself in Dublin comparatively soon conducting a rather similar performance on Bulleid's second 'C-C' design, with an even more critical audience including the Chief himself?

Unfortunately, the next day I was sent out and so missed the first move of No 36001 after all, but under her own steam. No 36001 was moved off the Works without much more fuss, intending to get coal at the shed. She arrived in the middle road on the west side of the station without much fuss but wouldn't reverse again. With live conductor rails everywhere, this was no place for pinch bars, so she was picked up and towed on to the shed and then back to the Works.

When safely back in the Erecting Shop it seemed a good idea to have a look under the covers over the front of the sleeve valves and their oscillating gear. The unsolved cause of the suspicious bang the previous day lay revealed on No 1 bogie. A valve rod had buckled and broken under a high compression load, just what many of us had feared. 'Water hammer' had almost certainly wrought the damage – and at the time the locomotive had not moved more than its own length! *(One thing Click fails to mention in his text anywhere is that No 1 bogie had, when undergoing a trial in Brighton Works using steam from an external source, been reversed before coming to a complete rest. The result was a jumble of rods and seizure. The faulty parts were quickly repaired/ replaced and Bulleid was evidently none the wiser. But it was a fact that most of the subsequent bogie trouble affected No 1 bogie. Was there then some weakness in the repaired machinery, or as has also been suggested, was the position of No 1 bogie under the boiler/ smokebox – the heavier and hotter end of the engine – also therefore under greater stress? The latter statement is of course pure conjecture, although what is known for certain is that at no time during the subsequent trials with No 36001 was a complete bogie exchange carried out with spares from the incomplete machines of the type. KJR.)*

As mentioned at the start of this series, the papers we have had access to were not in any order; they consist of several drafts, sometimes of the same topic and are also clearly missing sheets on occasion. As a result, attempting to conjoin what may have been a complete manuscript is difficult, to say the least. It is appropriate then to continue with No 36001, taking both a political and practical perspective.

No 36001 on paper and in practice

The correspondence between the Railway Executive and the Southern Region about the 'Leader' is rather interesting now in three ways. It shows how Bulleid's freedom was being questioned l more and more; and how, in the end his every move was vetted at the Kremlin: the one at 222 Marylebone Road. It also shows the clumsy way in which the Executive worked at that time. As the story unfolded department after department got drawn in, adding their own contributions to what was to be the 'Leader's 'pyre'.

For the first few months after Nationalisation, Riddles, Bond and Cox must have had their hands full settling into their new environment, testing the powers vested in them, setting up committees, working towards standards for locomotives, carriages and wagons, getting the Interchange Trials going and generally making visits to Works here, there and everywhere, seeking co-operation and trying hard not to be seen to be wielding the big sticks put into their hands. It would be natural, as well, to find them gauging the whereabouts, nature and strength of any opposition, or possible future embarrassments. Bulleid doubtless looked a likely source! *(JGC's exact words.)*

Early on, they would have also surveyed the various Regional Building Programmes which were in place from Company days and either in progress or too late to stop. Looking at the Southern, they would certainly have had grave misgivings about the five 'Leaders' authorised from 11 September 1946.

On 22 November 1948 Riddles wrote to "My dear Elliot" (the Chief Regional Officer at Waterloo), under the heading "New 0-6-6-0 Steam Tank Locomotives" making "one or two points which I consider important and on which I should like to have your views". Pointing out that individual costing of locomotives had not been a Southern practice, he went on to ask Elliot to arrange for:

> 1. A daily log for each of the five engines, showing work performed and the mileage run.
>
> 2. A daily record of running shed attention and repairs carried out with information regarding issues of lubricating oil.
>
> 3. A record of running shed repairs and examinations.
>
> 4. Individual records of costs of repairs or alterations in Main Works.

"Coal consumption will, of course, be an important point but this aspect of the matter will be covered by dynamometer car tests in due course." Possibly with visions of OVB doing something exotically non-standard over names and painting, he reminded Elliot that "in accordance with R. E. Memo. M.137" (of 3/5/48), proposals for the names of new locomotives are required to be submitted to The Railway Executive. A Committee is dealing with this matter in a general way and will shortly be making recommendations but as these engines are at the moment known as the 'Leader' class, you

Seen from behind the official photographer, 'the great and the good' are posed in front of No 36001 at Eastleigh on 28 June 1949. Note all the end doors of the engine are closed for the photographer; JGC makes reference to a design drawing showing the engine fitted with fixed windows in the driver's side doors. One disadvantage of the machine was that during shunting movements, the door had to be open for the driver, who, if he looked outside, risked being dangerously close to structures.

will no doubt have some particular names in mind and I shall be glad if you will submit your proposals as soon as possible." This letter concluded, "As these engines are mixed traffic types, I presume you are arranging for them to be painted black and lined in accordance with the decision conveyed in my letter of 26 April 1948, to Mr Bulleid, copy of which was sent to you." All a bit heavy by today's standards but very much in the idiom of the time.

Riddles wrote personally to Bulleid a fortnight later and was sent the following reply on 3 August, though Bulleid was clearly irked a little at having to write to confirm a conversation. "Dear Riddles, I informed you verbally that this locomotive is not yet in service. Your request for records has not been overlooked and as soon as the locomotive is delivered to traffic they will be kept and sent to you." It was signed Oliver Bulleid. (JGC adds in parenthesis: From this we are to assume that authority for the project was in effect now in the hands of Riddles and in many ways, this would indeed make sense. We may assume then that Bulleid's authority had in effect ceased from 1 January 1948 although he was retained to oversee the project until such times as the engines might enter traffic.)

Elliot was now acting as postman again and immediately replied to Riddles agreeing about the proposed costing, promising to write "shortly" about names and saying, cheerfully, "As these are Mixed Traffic Engines they will of course be painted black and suitably lined and I think they will look very well."

When No 36001 came out and started failing almost daily it was decided not to get the Testing section involved but to send draughtsmen out on her; after all they had done the design work, and it would be very good for them to see life out in the raw – for the first time in too many cases. It brought some of them down to earth with a bump long overdue. Nevertheless, it was a bitter blow to me not being involved, but my chance would come later.

Midnight oil was burned to get No 36001 to a BR Mechanical and Electrical engineers' conference held at Eastleigh on 28 June 1949. Everyone of note was invited and most turned up, where the 'Leader' was plainly the 'piece de resistance'. The trip from Brighton the previous day had been with a 'K' class 2-6-0 as a 'buddy' in case of a problem, or problems developing, but all went well, No 36001 keeping just a wisp of her own steam on all the way. Official photographs were taken shortly after the party arrived in reserved accommodation on the 8.30am from Waterloo. Many of the most senior VIPs always tended to group themselves at the centre.

It had really been touch and go getting No 36001 to Eastleigh for its important first official inspection and a team of foremen and fitters worked all the previous night. Bulleid had got the canteen ladies to lay on a midnight supper and a local agency photographer to record the event. On an occasion like this, OVB was completely without 'side' – for want of a better word. Everyone present would have treasured the rare personal contact they made that night, but as his 'Leader' ran into more and more trouble OVB found himself fighting a losing battle from which he eventually had little option but to withdraw. (In this last sentence we have at last confirmation from a 'man in the know' of exactly the opinion several writers have come to in the past, and without having the benefit of JGC's knowledge or experience. Indeed, I recall when I raised this very question with him, 'Do you think 'Leader' was dragging Bulleid down with it?', I was totally lambasted by him. At the time and still now I have not changed my opinion; my intention has always been to try and 'explain' the man, and not to condemn him. KJR.)

Back at Eastleigh, No 36001 behaved herself well. She was in steam and Riddles moved her in the yard and was said to have described the engine 'an unqualified success' by someone who should have been reliable and claimed to have heard him say so...perhaps he did. (Unfortunately, nowhere does JGC identify this individual.) Unfortunately, by now No 36001 was referred to in some traffic quarters as the 'Bleeder'. Riddles, I think, was never so ungentlemanly. (The unfortunate nickname came about due to an assumption as to how much the project had, and indeed still was, costing.)

However, the return journey, made alone, ran into trouble at Barnham though she was still able to get home running on five out of her six cylinders. Attwell and I went up the stairs to the Works boiler shop – over the footbridge by the main signal box to the other side of the main line as she arrived back. Her white tyres (which always made a locomotive look distinctive to me) were still clean.

Shortly afterwards, the 'Leader' began trials from Brighton, rather as No 2039 had, occasionally getting in more than one trip a day. However, reliability was poor. OVB's office faced away from the station with its constant noise, but the corridor outside did overlook the platform and I think he stood with [with whom?] on occasions as they would watch No 36001 start off on her first Victoria trip, via Lewes, East Grinstead and Oxted.

The view Mr Bulleid would have had from near his office at Brighton with No 36001 on a trial departing the station.

I saw her accelerating very nicely towards Falmer Bank. I was on holiday that day and cycled from Lee to Woldingham where the signalman told me she was returning to Brighton from Oxted having been 'short of steam'. I got there in the nick of time to find everyone very hot and dejected; and on impulse, shot out and bought a dozen ice- creams down the road. I was only gone a few minutes, but in that time so had the 'Leader'. I got very funny looks walking back, trying to give these rapidly melting things away, and most got dumped in the gutter. 36001's troubles weren't over then, for there was a pantomime getting water for her further down the line. (This was due to the Central Section water columns being too low for the high filler point on No 36001. Harry Attwell tells the story of how they had to carry a flexible extension, but which usually resulted in everyone getting drenched.– KJR.) They could have done with the ices!

The next day it was decided to go to Victoria again, on the same timing and with the same load – eight bogies. This time I decided I'd ride straight to Oxted, find out how she was doing and choose a good spot. "She's to stop here" I was told, without at the time understanding the significance of those few words. She duly arrived, having done a good deal better than the day before and, blowing off, hooked off and ran round. Only years later (in 1961) did I find out what had really happened that day. Wallace, whose job I took over after the poor man died of leukaemia, had occasion to ring 'The Kremlin' (meaning the headquarters of the Railway Executive at 222 Marylebone Road) and to speak to 'our man there', Butler, and said, "by the way if you could nip over to Victoria you might just be in time to see the 'Leader' arrive. Goodbye". Butler rushed out straight into R C Bond, who said, "I'll come too". Fate then took a hand, because in the corridors of power they overtook Rudguard, the Chief Motive Power Officer. "I'm not having that THING coming to London" he cried, and disappeared rapidly whence he had come, to see to it. Butler always felt guilty about the incident. 36001 never did visit London; though 36002 and 36003 got as far as New Cross Gate where they lodged for a while, only partly finished, before authority came to drag them back to Brighton for cutting up.

We might ask exactly why it was Rudguard was so adamant No 36001 was not to visit London. In my original books on the 'Leader' topic I had always maintained the intention was that Bulleid might prove his engine to the many doubters, but the trip was cancelled to avoid the risk of a failure and consequent disruption within the London area. Indeed, that may very well still be the case. But what I was unable to answer at the time and which JGC similarly fails to explain is why Rudguard took the view he did. With JGC's information it appears one of two situations came into play; firstly Bulleid may not after all have been directing the trials at all and a London test was on the shoulders of the testing staff, many of whom were still loyal to Bulleid, in addition we have the situation where human nature (pride) comes into being and for their own sake these same engineers wanted to prove that they were capable of running the engine to London and return. Presumably it would then have retired to Stewarts Lane for servicing – and that would certainly have made for some interesting photographs as well! Bringing Rudguard back into the frame again, we might even ask whether his views actually represented the privately held views of the CME hierarchy that prevailed at Marylebone? Perhaps so, for it will be recalled that a further attempt to visit London was never made. It was also slightly unusual for a steam engine trial to visit a London terminus anyway.

Excepting of course the 1948 interchange trialsl all other tests from, I think we can safely say, every locomotive workshop with a new design were initially local trips in that immediate area. With Marylebone clearly appraised of the none too successful test runs of 'Leader' to date perhaps Rudguard's attitude can be explained by this alone. JGC does not appear to analyse the events of the day anywhere in his text which is a pity as his views may even have afforded more of an insight. Whatever, and perhaps even whoever, it would have been an interesting logistical exercise to pass the 'cancelling' message from Marylebone to the Southern Region and then to disseminate it presumably by the Region's management down to the relevant control office and thence to the signal boxes along the route. KJR.

Meanwhile it appears also that Riddles was clearly not happy and changed his approach in his written correspondence. On 19 (October – ? 1949) he sent a 'tight' letter to S B Warder at Brighton. However Warder was not there – but Smeddle (ex-LNER) was. *(Robert Alfred Smeddle had been appointed Assistant Mechanical and Electrical Engineer for the Southern Region in 1949. In 1951 he moved as MEE to the Western Region at Swindon.)* Warder somehow (but that was what clerks are for) endorsed the letter for Smeddle's attention ASAP! Riddles had said, "The interpretation which Mr Bulleid has put on my requests … is not quite what I had in mind …and it is essential that I should have a full account of its (meaning No 36001's) performance and history since it was first turned out of the erecting shop. Will you, therefore, please gather together the information which you will have available … and send it to me at your early convenience." The first report was to be from day one to the end of September with monthly information "thereafter". On expenditure he asked for a "brief note" showing what No 36001 had cost up to the time it emerged, what had been spent on the remaining four, and how much 'alterations, etc.' had so far cost on the first locomotive. It was perfectly plain that Riddles (wise man?) was going to have chapter and verse on this one. *(The words 'wise man' and question mark are those of JGC.)*

Eight days later Warder sent off a summary of the "experience with the first 'Leader' engine from the time of her initial trip on the 22 June up to 30 September last". It had run 2,200 miles. *(There is an amount in the previous paragraphs that we cannot leave without making further comment. Firstly, the behaviour of Bulleid and where I don't think we can do anything other than say he was being 'evasive'. Riddles had every right to ask as he did and, having not received the response he expected, he was probably left with little alternative other than to go behind Bulleid's back. But this was not an easy thing to do, as likely it would create difficulty both at the time and subsequently. It also put Warder – and/ or his clerk – in a difficult position, Smeddle too perhaps. . We are not party to any discussions that might have taken place subsequently between the named individuals but what becomes ever clearer are Bulleid's attempts at fending off questions over his 'Leader', fearful perhaps that the truth would out. We are left with the inescapable conclusion that already Bulleid must have known that in the design of No 36001*

he had gone a step too far and yet who could blame the man for wanting to prove it had all been worthwhile. Success it must have seemed to Bulleid was always, 'just around the corner'. This is almost the only reference to R A Smeddle's time on the Southern Region and perhaps other than being aware of what was going on, he does not appear to have played any significant part in SR motive power during his short tenure. Finally, we should mention that at intervals throughout the JGC text, there are references he makes to having copies of correspondence. If this still survives, it has not been found and we are left with the quotes made both here and elsewhere in this text by JGC and unfortunately like Warder's summary, ie not the complete draft. KJR.)

'The Great Grey Galloping Sausage'

Any subsequent trials from Brighton with No 36001 are not referred to by Click; instead we move forward to the summer of 1950 with No 36001 at Eastleigh and JGC taking part in the dynamometer trials, although just before this he adds an interesting comment: Due to the difficulties with obtaining water for No 36001 on the lines from Brighton, some months earlier, when it was proposed to operate 36001 on the Brighton to Bournemouth through service, I was charged to measure up every water column between those points – a wretched job in mid-winter and especially single handed – I found most would cause difficulties of a similar kind except that is at Southampton Central. *(So we now know for the very first time one of the first duties the engine was intended to take….KJR.)*

For the dynamometer car tests at Eastleigh I usually rode in the fireman's cab of No 36001 and kept darting into the bunker to tip weighed bags of coal out on to the shovelling plate as required. At least this time I didn't have the miserable job of filling the sacks. At Eastleigh the engine turned on the triangle behind the shed that had been put in during WW2 in case the turntable or the main shed exit were bombed. *(Elsewhere JGC recalls No 36001 being shunted at Eastleigh by the very design it had been intended to replace – an 'M7' tank. KJR.)*

In the process of being shunted at Eastleigh, and by an M7 tank of all things!, JGC comments the Leader cab was ergonomically designed in favour of the driver.

No 30853 in the process of passing a stationary No 36001 waiting in Platform 2 at Eastleigh. It was a couple of seconds after this that the driver of the 'Lord Nelson' displayed a rude gesture in the direction of JGC – or was it aimed at No 36001?

For the first trial from Eastleigh, 'Leader' took the dynamometer car through to the north end of Eastleigh station where we waited for a passenger service hauled by No 30853 *Sir Richard Grenville*, to set off for Waterloo. I recall the driver of the 'Nelson' giving what I construed a rude sign indicative of the general feeling there. *(Likely towards the design of 'Leader' and how the fireman might be trapped in his compartment should the engine overturn. KJR.)*

The trials involving No 36001 also included a comparison with Maunsell 'U' class 2-6-0 No 31630. The car used was also the one that had streaked down Stoke bank at 126mph behind A4 Pacific No 60022 *Mallard* in 1938. We went most evenings from Eastleigh up the long drag at 1 in 250 and then on to Woking.

We then propelled the car down to Guildford from Woking to turn on the shed there. Nightly, I was in the fireman's cab lugging hundred weight bags of coal out of the coal space. Steaming was never free and some trips ended in defeat. Loads were gradually increased, and we always listened for sounds of mechanical irregularity. One night near Fleet there was a *crescendo* of new sound which then abated. Dutifully I made my way to the front to report only to find that we had just overtaken a 'T14' Paddlebox 4-6-0 which had attempted to have a race with us. What a sight that would have been in the half light! With only half a central cab we were blind to the 'double-breaster'!

On one of the trials later in the week, R G Jarvis rode with us and came into the fireman's cab to show willing.

However, unaware of the strict rota we had established for cooling our backs in the open door, he occupied that position continuously, so we were even hotter than usual. After we arrived in the Woking reception sidings, the loco and dynamometer car were detached and moved forward to await an opportunity to cross over and propel the car down to Guildford where both would be turned. In the dark, we shot through Worplesdon very swiftly indeed, driving from No1 end now and looking over the dynamometer car roof and beside the clerestory. The joke was on us because when we stopped just into the tunnel beyond Guildford station and got the dummy to reverse out, and into the loco depot, she wouldn't go over – this time not due to a fault in the reversing gear but instead a more basic shortage of steam – we had used it all on that mad dash from Woking. There was nothing for it but to put more coal on and wait for the blower to get pressure up again. I remember thinking on the way down, 'let's cut our losses and go on towards Portsmouth': what would the chain of events have been….the idea of 130 tons of great grey galloping sausage 'running away on right line' and propelling the terror struck E.& NE. regional crew in their dynamometer car hardly bears contemplation. Several of us would certainly have been looking for new employment. After about five long and very hot minutes, we succeeded in reversing. Then a look round the loco on shed showed that the mechanical lubricator driving gear at No1 end had broken at a weld in a way that did neither its designer nor its welder any credit. The return test was cancelled and No 36001 was left behind but the stock was worked back with us aboard. Ken Briggs, Doug Yarney and I went back next day to fit new parts sent from Brighton. We worked back light and very generously I was allowed to ride 'up front.' It was an unforgettable trip in bright moonlight, made very quietly and altogether without incident at a steady 50mph with a faster burst through Winchester. The ride was superb, with every wheel beat audible from end to end; as clear an indication of what might have been as I was indeed to see.

No 36002 was very nearly completed on the day that work was stopped on her and the other three. I got the news at lunchtime from an apprentice I knew and though not altogether surprised, I clearly remember the dismay that I felt. No 36001 was in a lot of trouble at the time, which, it was felt, was due to manufacturing problems overcome in the second locomotive and a plea was made from Works level to let testing go on with No 36002 in place of the first loco. I don't think the overall result would have been much different myself.

We believe JGC was involved in most, if not all, the trips from Eastleigh, in which case he would certainly have known of this occurrence' although not mentioned specifically in the located text; the occasion when the crank axle of No 36001 fractured on the northbound approach to Micheldever. The engine returned cautiously to Eastleigh with the axle falling into two pieces when the bogies were subsequently lifted. Despite this setback, Riddles – who would certainly have been informed – instructed a replacement be fitted and the trials continue.

No 36001 is almost ready to leave on a trial to Guildford via Woking. On the ground is the Traffic Inspector and behind him, fitter Doug Yarney is talking to Alistair Lawson of the Brighton Testing section, who was in overall charge. One of the Dynamometer staff is standing with his head out of the cab, which clearly indicates how precarious such a position might be on the move. Later on, they had a visit from a somewhat shorter official from Brighton, who opened the same door as the engine trundled through Eastleigh station in the small hours having returned from Guildford. He was immediately instructed to 'shut the door' by the driver as his front window was steaming up! He did so but only succeeded in shutting his head in the door in the process…

Guildford in the daytime. By rights No 36001 should never have been see here in daylight but this was the occasion when the 'great grey galloping sausage' had failed due to a broken weld to the mechanical lubricator driving gear at No1 end. In this view however, the fitter is attending to something at No 2 end. *Ron Pocklington collection*

With work stopped, No 36002 was stored at Brighton outside the old Copper shop before leaving for Bognor with No 36003 to go into store there. They simply had to be got out of Brighton shops for any other work to be done. When it became known they were at Bognor, the number of curious visitors caused another move, this time to New Cross Gate, where the Railway police soon became involved, when brasswork and copper piping started to disappear, though because they were not complete, nobody could say precisely what had been there in the first place! The two were later towed back to Brighton and cut up there. No 36004 got little further than having its boiler fitted to the main frame, so this was put on to an old carriage underframe and sheeted over until wheeled indoors again for eventual cutting up. Erection of No 36005 never started.

JGC also comments on the works plate that is known to been cast but never fitted to the engine; two fettled but unmachined castings were discovered in a cupboard at Brighton. One I filed up, painted and sent to OVB but it seems not to have survived. Had this appeared on 'Leader's side there would have been ructions, to say the least. It might be thought a bit naughty on Granshaw's part but I know just what must have taken place. In Dub in OVB told me to get the plates made and put my name on it. It was a pretty way of saying 'thank-you' but Granshaw took him literally and got them made in such a way as to 'win' his feud with Cocks! So far as I know, this, and one other example, is all that is left of the 'Leader' programme besides one of 36001's number plates that lies besides me now. *(The 'makers' plate referred to by JGC but of course never carried, was sold at auction a few years ago, reaching a four-figure sum – the present writer dropped out of the bidding as it went over the 'one thousand pounds' mark. One [of the two] 'smokebox' plates from No 36001,– possibly the one once owned by JGC, is on display at the National Railway Museum. It is not known if the second plate from the same engine survived. A smokebox plate from No 36002 is also known to be in private hands and was seen by the writer some years ago. Finally, Harry Frith [ex-Eastleigh Erecting shop Foreman] had one of the whistles from No 36001 stood on a plinth on his fire hearth for many years. KJR.)*

JGC concludes his account of 'Leader' with a frustrating statement which can now be elaborated upon; A book could be written of 'Leader' stories but I also recall one tranquil summer's night slipping down through Winchester under a brilliant moon and going a good deal faster than we were allowed. The ride was perfect, just the diddly-dum of the rail, perfect visibility; one could be forgiven for thinking the dream was a reality.

The 'Leader's swan song came on 2 November 1950. I was not there. 36001 somehow managed to haul 480 tons up to Basingstoke. Something to do with a big engine demanding a big train? One thing is sure though. Some of the sparks put up that night must have beaten the Sputnik into earth orbit.

Next time: other footplate and locomotive experiences, Rugby and the 'Irish Leader'.

With the almost complete No 36002 in the background, the boiler and frames of the incomplete No 36004 stand sheeted over outside Brighton works.

No 36001 did not take long to make steam as the grate area was large compared with the volume of water in the boiler. Full pressure could be got from cold in not much over two hours but a lot of smoke would result and damage to the brick lining of the firebox occurred due to differential expansion. The engine is seen here on the disposal/ coaling roads at Eastleigh. The height of the partly disassembled water column indicates how refilling water on the engine was not easy almost everywhere on the Southern. No 36001 steamed for the last time in November 1950 after which it was stored until the inevitable decision came from Marylebone that the project was to be cancelled. The engine was broken up at Eastleigh works the following year.

A Southern 15-ton 'pillbox' brake van, no S55677, seen at Branksome Pottery siding, probably sometime during the 1970s. This was one of 50 such vans built in 1934 to SR Diagram 1581 – a lighter version of the standard 25-ton vehicle and most were allocated to 'local' duties such as this post-Nationalisation. The rather 'thin' wash of BR light grey paint is degrading to reveal SR brown with red ends beneath – including the original 1934 'SR' letters, but apart from the number plate on the solebar the van appears almost anonymous. Even the 'local use' board below the lettering appears blank. The writer of these notes saw the van at Branksome yard in 1967 and 1969 and the lettering was then rather more obvious – as were the red ends – but maybe he saw the other side which could have weathered differently. Unlike most of the 25-tonners, the sandboxes remain in position, together with the delivery pipes adjacent to the wheels. Beyond are two BR 'Presflo' cement wagons, to BR Diagram 1/272 but whether they delivered cement, powdered slate or some other product to the pottery is not known. The siding left the main line just east of Branksome station and headed north-west for several hundred yards, crossing Cromer Road and entering the pottery premises of Messrs Sharp, Jones & Company, branching into two at this point – the other siding is just visible in the roadway. The van would operate just between the pottery and Branksome Yard, in the centre of the Bournemouth West triangle, so did not travel far. The site of the pottery is now Poole Retail Park and only a small portion of the original works buildings now remain behind the park. *Len Tavender, notes by Mike King*

Southern Report
Southern Report Number 2
George Hobbs

⇄ Southern

report

Number 2

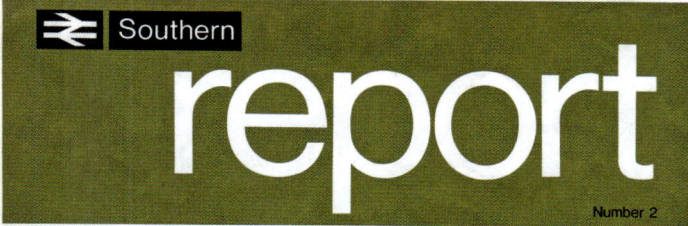

This is the Southern Region's second Report to its passengers. The first featured work on the track. This one specialises in stations. As before we try to explain our problems and how we intend to tackle them.

At last it's Summer

Forget that the lawn needs cutting and the house repainting.

Drop things and take a ride on the Southern.

We've plenty to offer—whatever your taste—and if you buy a cheap ticket you'll be surprised how much you can save.

Let's face it, there's no excuse for hanging round the house all summer long.

Not when there's a fast, comfortable Southern train to take you to no less than 40 seaside resorts along the South Coast.

And what a variety—Bognor Regis . . . Bournemouth and its long sandy beaches . . . Brighton and the Royal Pavilion and attractive Georgian architecture . . . Broadstairs home of Charles Dickens—you can still see his house . . . Folkestone, Dover and the White Cliffs . . . Eastbourne and Beachy Head . . . Hastings with its ruined castle, its fishermen and its funicular railway . . . Herne Bay . . . Ramsgate — where "Dreamland" specialises in exotic "fun" machines . . . Poole, Portsmouth and Southsea . . . Swanage and Seaford . . . Weymouth and Worthing . . . the Isle of Wight . . . and so the list goes on.

But maybe the thought of sea, sand, crowds and toffee apples does not appeal to you.

In that case there's always the beautiful countryside of the Southern England.

Sussex can boast of its Downs and all the contrasts of thickly wooded slopes and miles of rolling grassland — try starting from Hassocks . . . Hampshire, mild in its farmlands, grand in its New Forest —from Brockenhurst . . . Kent, famed for its orchards and oast-houses—from Otford . . . Surrey with Box Hill and miles of rambling heathland —from Dorking.

Or how about all the gardens and parks in which the Southern abounds? Here are a few with some fare examples.

Kew Gardens—*everyone* must have heard about Kew—with its open air plant museum and 250,000 different species of trees and shrubs. From Waterloo to Kew Bridge costs only 5s. return, from Dartford 10s. and from Haywards Heath 16s.

Don't forget the artificial lake—one and a half miles long—at Virginia Water. Constructed in 1746 and set in the south eastern corner of Windsor Great Park, a 9s. return ticket from Waterloo will take you there.

The Gardening Centre at Syon Park is a great attraction for gardeners and non-gardeners alike. Combined rail and admission tickets from Waterloo cost only 10s. —14s. from Orpington and Redhill.

Or how about Chessington Zoo with its 65 acres and 1,500 animals, a summer circus and an amusement park? Combined rail and admission tickets are 10s. from Waterloo, 16s. from Dartford and 16s. from Orpington.

And there's plenty of history on the Southern as well. Take Windsor Castle, for instance, where there is a half-hourly train service from Waterloo (fare 10s.) throughout the day. It's a 50 minute journey and gives you plenty of opportunity to wander around at leisure. And trains back are at the same frequency.

And, of course, there's Canterbury cathedral where Thomas Becket was murdered 800 years ago this year and where, during the summer months a festival of entertainment and religious events is being

staged. Return tickets from Charing Cross or Victoria cost 24s., from Bromley South 18s. and from Dartford 16s.

Besides all these opportunities to enjoy yourself, Southern Region's three Divisions are also running excursion trains at exceptionally low fares. On the South Eastern they will run on Wednesdays, and Sundays from London to the Kent Coast, while the Central are operating one-fare excursions—you pay the same amount from wherever you travel—to Bognor Regis and Littlehampton on Tuesdays, Wednesdays and Thursdays.

South Western's plans include all-inclusive tours from London and Bournemouth to the Isle of Wight where a coach tour is laid on. And there are also all-inclusive tickets being issued to view the liners at Southampton or a visit to Stonehenge. And all three Divisions run inclusive journeys to Hampton Court, Kingston and Windsor for river trips.

Don't forget that wherever you go you can usually get a cheap ticket between any two Southern Region stations.

We hope this has been of some help to you. So that's it, forget the paint and the lawnmower—AT LAST—IT'S SUMMER. GET OUT AND ABOUT.

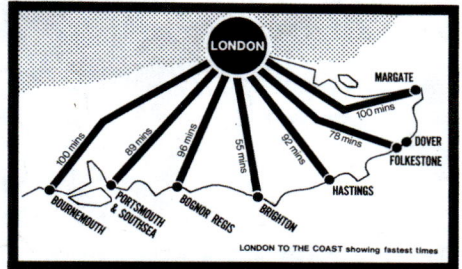

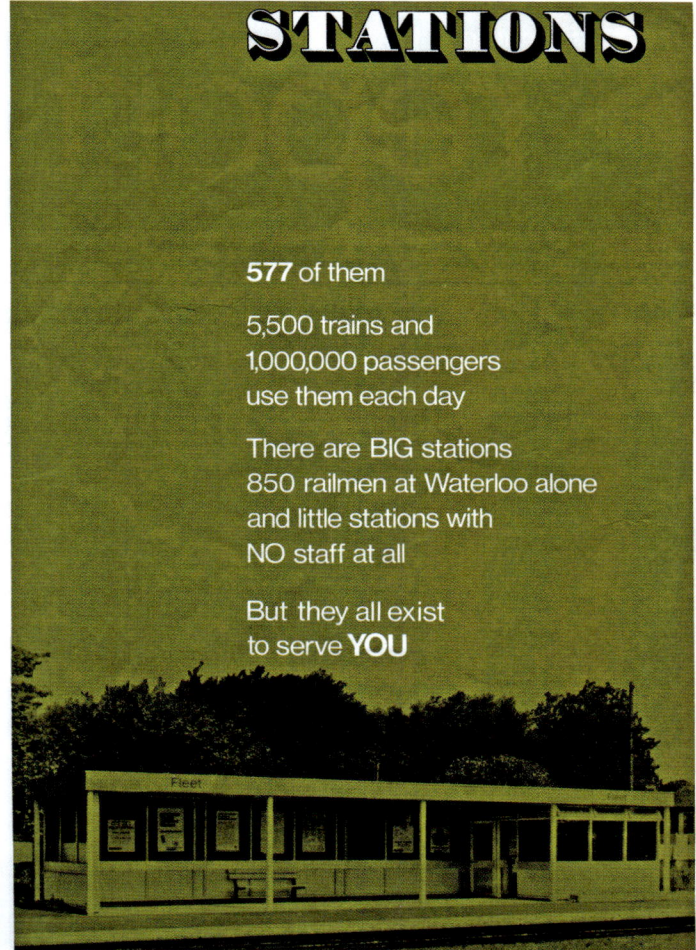

LONDON TO THE COAST showing fastest times

STATIONS

577 of them

5,500 trains and 1,000,000 passengers use them each day

There are BIG stations 850 railmen at Waterloo alone and little stations with NO staff at all

But they all exist to serve **YOU**

In the early 1970s the press severely criticised the Southern Region for overcrowded trains and service disruptions. In many ways such criticism mirrored the situation when the Southern Railway was carrying out its suburban electrification in the 1920s. In those days, Sir Herbert Walker, the Southern Railway's General Manager, recruited John Elliot as his Publicity and Advertising Assistant, and they set out to gain the Southern Railway passengers' support and sympathy. John Elliot showed how the difficult job of running a complex and busy railway was handled by the staff and management and asked for passengers' tolerance as the system was improved around them during the days of electrification, suburban sprawl and rapidly increasing traffic levels. Similarly, in 1970 the *Southern Report* was the railway's public relations fightback and this article discusses the second issue of the *Report* which travellers received that summer. (The first issue was earlier in the same year and may have handled the topic of cold weather and the attendant problems of ice-bound conductor rails.) The approach championed by John Elliot nearly fifty years before was still appropriate.

Parking your car at the station

Going by train's all right—once you're on the train. But you've got to get to the station first.

Lots of people walk it. Some go by bus and some by bike. But more and more go by car.

Some are kiss'n drive merchants with a wife to run them to the station and drive the car home again.

Others drive themselves and leave the car somewhere till they return. And there's the rub. Where to leave it?

Local residents don't take kindly to having a stranger's car dumped on the doorstep all day. The police can be even more positive. And every day the growing web of yellow lines becomes more and more ominous.

Now the Southern Region is well aware of all this and doing its best to help the motorist. It's simple economics really: find space for him to leave his car and we can sell him a rail ticket—fail to find space and he often drives all the way.

And it helps to keep down road traffic in Central London and other congested places.

In fact, we'd like to do more than this and find room not just for commuters' cars but for all the others who want to travel by rail during the day. Like the wife who can drive but doesn't fancy coping with heavy traffic in city centres.

The problem is where to put them because cars, parked, take up loads of room.

It's been suggested we should build car parks over railway lines—but that's frighteningly expensive and the charges to park in them would be pretty frightening too.

The new system of dealing with freight in large amounts at big modern depots instead of in penny packets at dozens of stations has left us with lots of empty goods yards, sidings and disused coal yards.

Unfortunately, however, the places where there's land to spare don't always coincide with where people want to park their cars. And at some places where there's a desperate need for more car parking space there just isn't any land to spare at all.

Don't forget that to turn even an already flat piece of former goods yard into a car park does cost money. Anyone who's had their drive resurfaced will know what we mean. In our case, it often involves removing tracks, buffers, huts, signals and other bits and pieces, perhaps levelling part of the ground, laying down hardcore and asphalting the lot. O.K., it's no Aswan Dam, but it can work out as high as £150 at times for each car space.

So far the Southern has managed to find room for 9,100 cars at 377 of its 577 stations. There are six other parks at Smitham, Streatham, Surbiton, Epsom, Meopham and Pulborough which are privately owned and run for Southern Region. There are plans to provide over 5,500 more spaces at over 50 stations at a cost of £500,000.

But that's long term. In the short term the Region is providing 791 spaces at 25 stations for about £137,000 within a matter of months.

Biggest project is at Guildford where 343 spaces are being provided for £56,000. At the other end of the scale is Cobham where 25 spaces are being provided for only £105. Other places include Barnehurst, Petts Wood, Canterbury West, Crowhurst, Etchingham, Gravesend, Maidstone East, Newington, Rainham, Sevenoaks, Shortlands, Sidcup, Staplehurst, Tunbridge Wells Central, Bookham, Eastbourne, Esher, Farncombe, Godalming, Staines, Poole, Woking, Swanley, Crowborough and Hook.

We're sorry if your station isn't included in this list but, as we've said so often, there are 577 stations on the Southern and we can't improve them all at once.

In Southern Region car parks there is a reasonable daily charge, but if you get a quarterly season ticket, you can cut the cost by nearly half.

With the stretch of an arm

Getting in and out of some car parks is now controlled by automatic barriers. Southern Region has several where, with the stretch of an arm out of the window, motorists can gain easy access.

These are being rapidly introduced at many stations and at the latest count there were 19 on the region. This one is at Richmond, others are at Leatherhead, Three Bridges, Dorking, Dover Priory, Sevenoaks, Staplehurst, Petts Wood, West Malling, Otford, Headcorn, New Eltham, Maidstone East, Twickenham, Hampton Court, Bournemouth, Cobham, Farnham and Wokingham.

Others are planned for Shoreham, Purley, Paddock Wood, Bexley, Hildenborough, Gravesend and Longfield.

You either put cash in the machine to get in the car park or use a specially sensitised season ticket.

Key Posts save trouble

This post can mean the difference between having to hunt for a parking space or the luxury of driving straight into one.

We have provided 10 similar posts at Sevenoaks as an experiment for motorists who want a space which only they can use.

Each motorist holds a key to unlock his post (pictured here) which stops anyone else using the car space behind it. He then lowers the post to drive his car in. When raised afterwards it automatically locks.

The post also serves as an excellent anti-thief device and gives the key-owner the best space in the car park nearest the station entrance.

So successful has the idea been although the cost is half as much again as the normal parking fee—all spaces were sold out within two days—that we are going to erect another six spaces at Etchingham and 10 at Bexley. And that's only a start. There'll be more.

We're smartening up our Stations!

Many of our stations are antique. You know it and we know it.

We've rebuilt a few stations, of course, and we're proud of those. And we've done a lot to smarten up many others.

Viewed solely from a purely practical point of view they are usually too big and too expensive to maintain. They are no longer what is wanted by the passenger or by ourselves.

The main reason for this is that most of the buildings are about 100 years old.

As a result we now have an enormous backlog of work. And we have an enormous number of stations to deal with—577. We can't knock them all down at once.

But it is becoming increasingly urgent that we do make a real start on a planned programme to bring them all up to date within a reasonable period.

We have suggested to the British Railways Board and the Ministry of Transport that we should think in terms of reconstructing or renovating 30-40 of the more important stations each year.

In addition to that there are about 130 small stations which want knocking down as they become due for major repairs and replaced with a small compact building.

In these cases the Region is using a very versatile system of building from factory-made parts known as "CLASP" and examples of this are already in existence at Fleet, Sunbury, Ashtead, Belmont, Crayford, Charlton, Belvedere, Aylesham, Slade Green, Hampton Wick, Berrylands and Catford.

Of course, in addition to the major projects there is also a continual need to repaint stations and carry out minor but pressing improvements.

To cover all this sort of work at stations, from the minor jobs to major reconstruction the Southern Region set aside £1.4m for work in 1970.

Already work at a large number of these stations has been completed or is nearing completion, including: Ashford (Surrey), Basingstoke, Godalming, East Croydon, Horley, Kingswood, New Cross Gate, Gatwick Airport, Ifield, Three Bridges and Bickley.

New stations completed so far include: Catford, Newington, South Bermondsey, Wool and Poole with Southwick and Teynham in progress and Rainham and Hampton Wick to come later.

Major improvements in progress—or shortly to start—include: Beckenham Junction, Blackheath, Rochester, Tonbridge, Broadstairs, Chislehurst, Elmstead Woods, Kent House, Swanley, Barnes, East Putney, Surbiton, Barnham, Oxted, Barnehurst, Epsom and New Beckenham.

Other major work planned for later includes Hither Green and Woolwich Arsenal.

Don't despair if YOUR station is not on this list. We can't improve all our 577 stations at once. But we know what's required and we will do it as soon as we can.

One of the Southern's new CLASP stations.

Comparison between *Southern Report No2* and the situation today reveals how much the railway has changed in the intervening period. The centre pages feature a photograph of a 4-VEP disgorging commuters by a CLASP (Consortium of Local Authorities Special Programme) station building as an example of the (then) latest main line rolling stock serving modernized passenger facilities.

The VEPs (Vestibule Electro-Pneumatic) were originally introduced for the stopping services on the Bournemouth line when it was electrified in 1967, with further batches duly displacing the 1930s BIL, HAL and LAV stock by mid-1971. While never glamorous, the VEPs proved to be reliable movers of rush-hour crowds on outer suburban and long-distance services across all three divisions of the Southern network for well over thirty years, and certainly earned their keep. Sadly, the passenger comfort level afforded by the slender cushions of a 4-VEP was not quite as high as a BIL, but the HALs were almost as spartan as their successors.

Southern Report No2 extols the modernity of the CLASP prefabricated station structures that were replacing out-of-fashion Victorian buildings in many country and suburban locations.

The 4-VEP in the centrespread is shown at the modernized Fleet station on the former LSWR main line between Woking and Basingstoke. CLASP structures were adopted by the Southern and, to a lesser extent, the Western regions on the grounds of economy. With hindsight these CLASP buildings were less than ideal, being generally disliked and lacking in character. Those at Fleet were demolished in 2013 and the rebuilt station opened in July 2014, with improved parking and bus interchange facilities. Although a 4-VEP has been restored to original rail blue livery with burnished metal insignia it seems unlikely that any remaining CLASP structures will be preserved for posterity or gain listed building status.

The inconvenience to passengers due to major works being carried out at the main London termini was also addressed in the *Southern Report*. On the penultimate page a photomontage of Victoria is shown with the massive mechanical train indicator board superimposed above what appears to be a pre-war 2-BIL, which was in its final year of service when the *Report* was issued and could well have left the station for the final time before the board was installed. Within twenty years a further onslaught on Victoria saw the demise of the train shed on the

East Croydon—before and after.

Fancy a job on the Southern?

To run the passenger side of its 577 stations the Southern Region needs 8,000 staff. In fact, there are 1,400 vacancies and the Region does the best it can with the 6,600 staff it has. Of these there are 5,500 uniformed staff working on the platforms and 1,100 in the ticket offices.

Four out of five passengers travelling on the Southern Region pass through one of the Region's London terminals. We are anxious to make these stations as attractive and as convenient as possible for all who use them.

This year, for instance, the Region will spend £330,000 on improving them. Here are details of some of these plans:

Cannon Street

Used by 77,500 passengers a day, Cannon Street is to have seven shops and a pedestrian walkway built on the disused forecourt.

But before the shops and walkway can be built, London Transport is having to strengthen the roof of their station so that it can carry the extra weight above and also enable Cannon Street to be made about 25 feet wider at this spot.

The walkway will be along the front of the station and will form the first stage in the City of London's plan to have an elevated walkway system running the whole length of Cannon Street, connecting southwards to the river and northwards to King William Street and the Bank. The rest of the walkway in Cannon Street depends, however, on the widening and rebuilding of the south side of Cannon Street.

The temporary walkway now in position across Cannon Street will also be replaced later with a permanent structure.

London Bridge

Used by 165,000 passengers a day, there is an urgent need to modernise London Bridge where some of the buildings are now being demolished.

This will allow a new bus station and bus aisle covered with a canopy to be provided by London Transport and improve interchange facilities.

Plans for the future include a new centralised ticket office and barrier line.

When removing some of the old buildings, ironwork structures, which have not seen the light of day for about 120 years, were revealed. The buildings were on the site of the original station opened in 1836 on the London and Greenwich Railway—the first public railway in London.

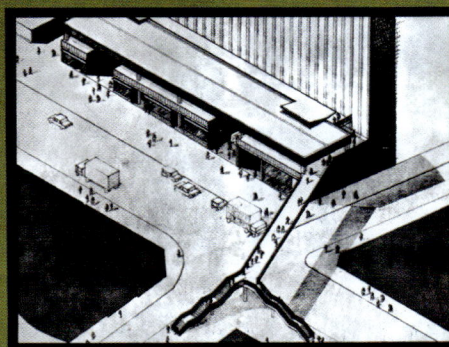

120 year old ironwork

A CAPITAL INVESTMENT!

Brighton side of the station and the installation of the current concrete raft and retail premises above the platforms, together with fully electronic train-display apparatus.

London Bridge station was also updated in the mid-1970s, although the predicted changes involving the new bus station and ticket office were on a different scale to the wholesale reconstruction project carried out to accommodate the enhanced Thameslink services during the past few years. The improvements described at Cannon Street have also passed into history as the latest redevelopment of the station, with the incorporation of new structures above the platforms, has seen the 1970s modernity swept away and replaced by yet another even more modern structure. Forty years appears to be the approximate lifespan for office accommodation in central London. Compared to the works at the other London termini the upgrade of Waterloo was remarkably sympathetic with the train shed retaining much of its airy atmosphere.

On the Brighton main line, the major station at East Croydon features on the centre pages and the before and after photographs show the brightly-lit booking hall as a far more welcoming place than its gloomy painted-wood predecessor.

Yet again the 1970s styling has not endured as the remodelling of East Croydon's facilities in the late 1990s saw stainless steel and glass displace the old buildings, and their cosmetically updated interior from the 1970s. The interchange with Croydon Tramlink on the street frontage now provides a welcome integration with local transport facilities; the taxi rank has been displaced to the east side of the station.

In the 1970s, with the aftermath of the Beeching report, the redeployment of redundant goods yards and siding space into more passenger-friendly car parks was seen as a big step forward and merits a full page in *Southern Report No 2*, with details being given of the new facilities and their provision across the region. The description of the removal of freight traffic to large modern depots has a hollow ring, as many of these have now suffered the same fate as the small local yards dating from the railway's early days. Even as late as 1970 the almost total shift away from non-passenger operations within the Southern area would have seemed highly improbable to the readership.

The final page adds what would now be regarded as politically incorrect language as the promotion of the 'touch

Victoria

Used by 17,000 passengers a day, Victoria station is having two giant train indicators—each nearly 40 yards long and thought to be the biggest in the world.

One of the indicators will be above the ticket barriers on the side used by Brighton trains at Victoria and the other on the side used by services to the South East.

By about August both will display identical information on 30 panels giving details of train departures from the station's 17 platforms and of main line arrivals. Information on Continental boat trains and Gatwick Airport services will also be displayed.

Each of the eight foot deep panels will show the platform number, time and destination of the next train with intermediate calling points.

Another improvement to Victoria, besides the painting of the roof, which is going on at the moment, will be improved gents' toilets on the Central side.

London Transport are also carrying out work at Victoria. They are building a canopy in the forecourt to cover people waiting for buses and are improving interchange facilities.

Waterloo

Used by 200,000 passengers a day, Waterloo, Southern Region's biggest and busiest station is expected to have a new look by the end of the year.

A new centralised ticket hall and ticket office is being built on the site of the former "Long Bar", which closed last summer. A temporary "Thames Bar and Buffet" came into use at the Windsor line end of the station.

A new popular-priced restaurant—with decor and design based on ideas submitted by customers—is also to be built at Waterloo.

Stripping out the 'Long Bar'.

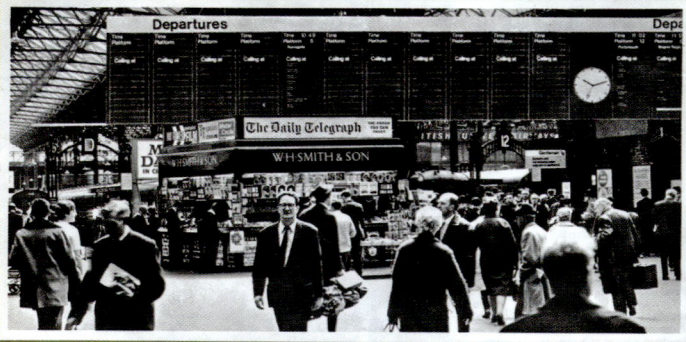

Impression of how new Victoria indicator will look

They're all here to help you!

Hostess

Besides adding a touch of beauty to the scene, Southern Regions' hostesses—Rail-Air and Rail-Sea—at Victoria, Gatwick Airport and Heathrow, do a grand job helping the public.

They are always on hand to give advice, assist with general inquiries and sort out any language problems.

Self help luggage trolleys

To make the transfer from train to car or bus easier—or vice versa—self-service luggage trolleys, on the supermarket style, are available at a number of Southern Region stations.

Placed on the platform or in the ticket hall, each trolley takes about three suitcases and also has room for small items of hand baggage in a separate basket in the front.

Engineering Maps

With all the engineering work we have to carry out each weekend—remember it's for YOUR benefit in the long run—weekend travel is sometimes disrupted.

To help you plan your journey well in advance we have placed a number of illuminated display maps of the whole of Southern Region at a number of stations.

Each Monday morning coloured arrows are put on the map showing where the big engineering jobs are taking place the following weekend. Red arrows indicate that trains are affected on the Saturday and green arrows on the Sunday. Black arrows mean the work goes on over the whole weekend.

Passengers who plan to travel over the "arrowed routes" can check train details with the station's information office or one of Southern's 13 telephone enquiry bureaux.

Check your week...

Published by British Rail Southern AD3400/A250/12570
Printed by The Oringport Press, Portsmouth.

of beauty' brought by the customer-facing hostesses on the Rail-Air and Rail-Sea services at the major stations would surely be frowned on now!

In 1970 my local station (Belmont on the Sutton to Epsom Downs branch) had just received its CLASP building but retained both of its tracks and platforms. Today the CLASP structure and the station staff are long gone. One track has been lifted and the single serviceable platform has a ticket machine, an Oyster card reader, a bike shed and a rudimentary shelter. Strangely this un-manned halt is in the Greater London area and adjoins a busy main road and bus route. No car park here – the goods yard was a quarter of a mile away – and the land was sold for a housing development.

Looking ahead another fifty years, one is left wondering how much of today's railway scene will remain in 2070. I am sure that the Southern atmosphere will linger on. Today 10-car class 377s are the new order on the Southern Metro lines but what will carry the commuters of the future?

Unintentionally Non-stop:
Caterham to Selhurst

Nicholas Owen

'Finally at rest'. *Courtesy the Croydon Advertiser*

We recently received the following courtesy of Nicholas Owen. It was indeed fortunate no injuries resulted although no doubt there would have been an internal Southern Region investigation. (Does anyone have anything further...?)

Nicholas writes, "As a follow up to the interesting letter in *SW49* from Geoffrey Pudney – who recalled seeing a runaway EMU going through Purley – here are more details of a most extraordinary incident.

"It was on 29 March 1974.The technicalities are tricky to understand, but it seems a motorman at the Caterham branch terminus left his EPB unit No 5323 with key in, and the electro pneumatic brake fully applied. Unfortunately, the brake managed to leak, and the handbrake hadn't been wound on. The unit ran away down the long, mostly downhill grade towards London (!). Quick-thinking signalmen along the line ensured level crossing gates were open, and no other train got in the way. It's estimated the runaway reached about 20mph. At Purley, junction with the main line – where Mr Pudney witnessed the driverless EPB going through – it's said a driver made an attempt to get aboard, but No 5323 was going a bit too quick for him. On she went, sailing through the always very busy East Croydon, heading inexorably towards the metropolis. Wise heads realised there was a solution. The unit was deflected on to the Slow Line approaching Norwood Junction, then on to a Selhurst depot approach road, before finally colliding with buffers and derailing when it reached a stub beside platform 1 at the Junction. You can still see the repairs done to the brickwork." (It was not a good day for accidents on BR as several hundred miles away at Glasgow, a driver passed a signal at danger, resulting in a head-on collision and two injuries.)

Station Architecture on the Chessington Branch

Stephen Spark

We were delighted to receive correspondence on the above topic from Stephen Spark. Originally submitted by him for 'Rebuilt', we rapidly came to the conclusion that it would be far better served as a stand-alone piece, which, having read it, I am sure you will agree; for two totally unconnected, contemporaneous images of the locations turned up, we think hitherto unseen, ...Ed.

This is best served cleaned up from the third line!

... a stand-alone piece, with which, having read it, I am sure you will agree; for two totally unconnected, contemporaneous images of the locations turned up. We think them hitherto unseen ...Ed.

Dear Kevin, it has taken me a while to catch up with *SW46* and those splendid images of Malden Manor, but if it is not too late I should like to add a few comments about the Chessington branch stations.

It's not quite true to state that "all four of the new stations displayed the same design of Chisarc cantilevered canopies". Nor were the stations identical at street level.

Malden Manor and Tolworth, the northernmost pair on the branch, were opened in May 1938. Their station buildings were finished in a novel form of rendering called 'Brizolite', which had been introduced to Britain from Germany by Bauhaus, its founder Walter Gropius. I have found no other references to the material being used for British railway stations, although it was employed in the detailing of some late-1930s cinemas.

The entrance to the new Tolworth station on opening day, 25 May 1938. Representatives from the Boroughs of Malden and Surbiton travelled in what was described as a 'special train' but without further detail given. The symbols on the flags are not known but Southern Railway and one of the Boroughs perhaps? The great and the good are present as well as at least two workmen, one on the extreme right and another putting the finishing touches to the canopy roof.

The crisp white render of the Brizolite, the elegant lines of the Chisarc canopies and the other concrete components combined to create an attractive, clean, modern image suitable for the Southern Electric. Gilbert Szlumper noted: "I like the Chessington line stations and look on them as an auspicious start."

However, in July 1938, just two months after the first two stations opened, chief engineer George Ellson told Eustace Missenden that the next pair, Chessington Court and Chessington Grange (renamed shortly before opening as Chessington North and Chessington South respectively), "will be faced with brick instead of 'Brizolite'". The GM asked: "Is this because the latter substance has not proved satisfactory? The appearance of the stations which have been finished is quite agreeable and it might be worthwhile keeping the others of the same external appearance." The answer was given in a conversation of which we have no record, but perhaps the additional cost of the rendering played a part in the decision. Nevertheless, if kept in good condition it can still look smart.

Chessington North and South were therefore left with a more subdued brick finish, though in his inspection report of 25 May 1939 Col Trench found that "the buildings are attractive in appearance". He also noted that South station, "has been provided with a special ARP shelter for about 30 persons, in concrete at platform level; at the North station the concrete subway is earmarked for the same purpose".

The second picture of Malden Manor shows the Chisarc canopies to great effect. Like Brizolite, the Zeiss-Dyckerhoff system of reinforced concrete shell construction originated in Germany in the mid-1920s, having first been used to build a planetarium for optical equipment manufacturer Carl Zeiss. In the UK, the system was licensed to T A Chisholm of Architectural Services Ltd (hence 'Chisarc'), with Berlin-based Dyckerhoff & Widmann (D&W) acting as consulting engineers. Ellson chose Chisarc for the Chessington branch platform canopies in June 1937, explaining that "this form of roof gives a clear platform without any intermediate supports and has the advantage of avoiding periodical expensive painting" (painting was subsequently found to be necessary, however). Ellson reassured Missenden that "this form of construction has been already adopted by the LMS Railway Company for a large timber shed with satisfactory results".

In December 1937, D&W wrote a rather pained letter to Chisholm protesting about the valance that the SR had insisted be added to the canopies. Apparently, there had been "long discussions" about it in various letters, as D&W felt that it was unnecessary, would spoil the look of the canopy (which it does) and prevent light reaching the back of the platform. "We got the impression that the Southern Railway engineers must have a serious reason when asking for this valance which is not yet known to us." If the SR insisted on this feature, D&W continued, "we still hope that it will be possible to convince the Railway Engineers to use a glass valance". The German consultants stressed that they wanted to do, "all in our power to make this first structure for the Southern Railway to a first class example of Chisarc construction".

In the following months there was a change of heart at Waterloo and in July 1938 Missenden reminded his chief engineer that, "for the stations to be built it was agreed that the ribs of the concrete platform roofs should be placed on the outside of the roofs which should be so designed as to obviate the necessity for a valance". Eighty years later you can still hear the sigh of relief from Messrs Dyckerhoff & Widmann!

The change was a great improvement visually, as the revised design of Chisarc canopy looks much 'cleaner' and lighter than the 1938 model. Recently, we have been given an opportunity to see the external ribs on the canopy roof, as in 2019 a public path was built behind the down platform at Chessington South.

This new ramp from platform to street level also affords an opportunity to see the unlovely back side of John Robb Scott's design. His stations on the branch were designed to be seen from certain angles only, preferably when brand new and free of 21st century damp stains, peeling paint, graffiti and ugly clutter. Behind the scenes, they look cheap and rather nasty – perhaps the Southern was trying to cut costs as construction estimates were exceeded. The pure lines of the Chisarc canopies aside, it is fair to say that in their neglected, unstaffed state the Chessington branch stations have not worn well.

Although there were 'milk ramps' at the stations and towers (but no equipment) for luggage lifts, the SR provided no alternative to long flights of steps at Malden Manor, Tolworth and Chessington North. On a recent visit to the line I saw people clearly struggling to get up and down those stairs, and it seems odd that stations designed for lifts in the 1930s are still waiting for them in the age of 'accessible transport'.

Ellson specified "a modern method of lighting designed to be in keeping with this type of roof, viz: Fluorescent Tubes". The higher first cost would be offset by lower running costs, Ellson assured his boss. The rather daring combinations of pink, amber, blue and white tubes must have added to the gaiety – what a pity we have no night-time colour images of this fairground attraction! Passengers had little time to enjoy the 'Chessington Illuminations', however, as shortly after the line opened, wartime blackout restrictions were imposed. In the daytime, portholes in the canopies (now all blocked off) and larger skylights helped dispel the image of railway stations as essentially dark and grimy places.

A word ought to be added about goods facilities. As all the stations between Motspur Park and Leatherhead Junction, apart from Chessington South, were going to be elevated, road-rail interchange was not going to be straightforward, and it seems to have been agreed at an early stage that only Tolworth and Chessington South would have goods yards. The former was provided initially with just a single siding, but two more roads were soon added as the yard was extended when more fill was brought in. There was talk, too, of a goods shed, but this seems to have been abandoned on grounds of cost and fear that it would abstract traffic from Surbiton. Attempts to get Charrington's, the coal merchants, to pay for the facilities were rebuffed, but they were provided anyway at the SR's expense.

Again Tolworth and the lift tower which has never fulfilled its intended purpose. When excavations were being made for the station, rocks 27 feet below the surface were found to be embedded with shells which the British Museum estimated to date back 20 million years.

Later, of course, Tolworth and Chessington coal concentration depots became important distribution centres in the final two decades of domestic coal traffic on the railways. Charrington's 'model' coal depot at Chessington opened in 1963 and survived until 1988. The site is now used by a company supplying peat and topsoil for gardeners, but it's quite possible that some of the tracks still survive, entangled within an inaccessible forest of birch and alder. Tolworth also lost its coal role, but today sees regular trains from Cliffe (Brett Marine), which bring in 130,000 tonnes of aggregates a year.

It is clear from the surviving records that the Chessington branch was built in some haste. The engineers had to face several unusual challenges, while the designers (emulating Mr Bulleid, perhaps!) seem to have been given a fairly free hand to try out innovative techniques and materials. Consequently, the route, its purpose and the designs of structures, goods facilities and stations were in a state of constant flux as the line was being constructed, evolving rapidly as one plan succeeded another. The fact that there was no as-built survey of Chessington South station and yard until 1947 shows how much got missed in the rush to get the line finished before the international political standoff exploded into war.

If the route had ever been able to reach its ultimate goal, shoehorning the Chessington line's three services an hour into the cramped and awkwardly sited station at Leatherhead would have presented a serious challenge. The station would surely have required a hugely expensive rebuilding, but I have found no reference to this ever being discussed. Perhaps Leatherhead was never more than an aspiration – but, if so, why would the Estate Department have sweated blood and money to buy, at inflated prices, parcels of land all the way through Malden Rushett and Epsom Gap into Leatherhead?

Malden Manor and its ilk were certainly ground-breaking at the time, but the war brought this surge of optimistic modernism to a halt. Peace brought only shortages, higher costs and austerity, so a lot of what came later was merely functional and utilitarian. We can only speculate about the architectural innovations that might have been introduced had the line progressed farther south. However, its failure to do so allows us to still enjoy Charles Driver's delightful polychrome 'neo-Renaissance' brick concoction for the LBSC, now a Grade II listed building.

Some final questions remain. How would Leatherhead station have been rebuilt? Did the encasing of steel bridges really help reduce maintenance and increase strength as claimed? Was the Chisarc system used for any other passenger stations in Britain? Does any solid evidence exist for the oft-repeated claim that the Royal Engineers built the unused embankment beyond Chessington South and how far did the track extend along it? When was the single-line bridge over Chalky Lane built and removed? If anyone knows, it will surely be a *Southern Way* reader!

Quoted passages above are from letters in The National Archives, ref RAIL 1188 116, except Col Trench's report, which is RAIL 1188/112.

Rebuilt
The Letters and Comments Pages

A full amount of correspondence again this month for which we are grateful. We start with a piece from **Richard Whitbread** reference David Austin and **Slip Coaches: SW47**. Richard Whitbread comments that on p99 David Austin refers, "…there was a slip at Caterham for Reading and Maidstone." Reference 11 is given. As Caterham is at the end of a branch this seemed odd and the original Kidner statement says "at Caterham Junction in 1861, the slipped portion dividing and working on slow to Reading and Maidstone." Caterham Junction was the then name for Purley which makes more sense. I assume the slipped coaches were taken to Redhill before being further divided for Reading (turn right) and Maidstone (turn left via Tonbridge and Paddock Wood).

Moving forward to p48 of **SW48**, "Unit 406 is on delivery with a non-mu fitted 33. I doubt if a) illuminated red tail blinds were recognised off the Southern Region at the time as indicating the rear of the train and b) that if the unit had not been commissioned then the electrics may well not have been functioning and the red tail blinds may well not have been illuminated. In which case an old style tail lamp was required!" Finally and still on **SW48**, this time p101, "… a Class 71 is

We are grateful to Bob Winkworth for the attached, showing what he thinks is the depot at Wimbledon following the demolition of the power station. No 4342 is engaged in a 'shunt' whilst other sets await their next turn of duty.

unlikely to have been at Waterloo but in fact E6025 is one of the wonderful go anywhere class 73s. Homer obviously nodded today!" *(We might add that Richard's name will certainly be recognised as the author of the excellent series on 'SR Electrics' started in SW a few issues ago. We are promised more from Richard in the near future – Ed.)*

Now from **Roger Macdonald** a literal change of direction. "The image of the train in Victorian/ Edwardian days arriving at **Whitwell – p62 SW49** – is in fact arriving from the direction of Merstone and not Ventnor West."

Next from Graham Southern who points out, "The picture outside Orpington carriage sheds struck me as being slightly unusual as the Victoria – Orpington service is coming in on the down fast line. Its normal path would have been on the down slow next to the carriage shed and into platform 6. The 7.59 Orpington – Victoria used the up fast, as did the following service (8.05'ish) which departed from platform one. The pictured service is also almost certainly off-peak by virtue of the fact that it is 4 cars."

Now from **Ray Grace**. "Dear Kevin, I have been an avid reader of Southern Way since issue No1 but this is the first time that I have decided to put pen to paper and comment. I particularly liked the piece on the east **Kent coalfield** in **SW48** because I lived in the Deal/Walmer area during my teenage years

Down stopper at Seaton Junction. No 30823 'S15' 4-6-0, more normally expected to be seen on freight or on a Summer Saturday relief, rolls into the station with a featherweight load.

between 1948 and 1960. From Easter 1953 until Summer 1960, I commuted to school in Ramsgate by train and, obviously, became very familiar with railway operations in the area.

I hope that a little bit of additional information concerning the operation of trains to/from Betteshanger colliery might be useful as I believe the operation to reverse the empty wagon train at Deal was very unusual, if not unique, in Britain as it involved a lengthy 'fly shunt' along a main line.

A bit of background; the layout at Deal consisted of the usual up and down platform roads but there was also a third, signalled, siding between them with entry/exit from both ends. The up line (from Sandwich) approached Deal on the level but at the Dover end of the station platform a significant (c1/100) gradient commenced. Empty wagon trains bound for the colliery approached from Sandwich, reversed, and departed towards Betteshanger (situated between Deal and Sandwich) where the only access was via a trailing connection into the 'down' line. There were also full loco facilities at Deal in the former loco shed which then was in use as a wagon repair depot.

For ease of description of the manoeuvre I will need to resort to a tabular format.

An empty wagon train with c30 wagons, usually in the charge of an 'N' class 2-6-0 or sometimes a 'Q1', approached the station on the 'up' line at some speed and as it entered the station the driver closed the regulator. As the wagons 'buffered up' the guard uncoupled his 'dance hall' brake van by leaning over the veranda end; he then applied the handbrake to bring the 'van

to a halt in the 'up' platform. The loco and train continued on up the hill to come to a halt beyond the siding points and the 'dummy' before reaching the advance starter signal.

The loco and wagons reversed into the siding and the loco uncoupled.

The loco then ran around, both the wagons in the centre road and the brake van in the 'up' platform, via the 'down' platform road and buffered up to the brake van. It then propelled the 'van at speed and released it to 'fly shunt' up the hill on the main line until it cleared the siding points and dummy. The signalman, by watching his track circuit lights, quickly cleared the points and signal so that the 'van free-wheeled by gravity on to the (now) rear of the wagons in the centre road.

In the meantime the loco reversed from the 'up' platform road and made its way to the loco facilities where it was turned and watered.

In due course the loco returned to the wagons and set off on the 'down' line for Betteshanger. This operation took place twice a day on most days.

I spent a lot of time at Deal station and was well known to the staff there having access not accorded to the public; like riding the 'van on some of these fly-shunts, hours on the footplate of the daily shunter (usually a 'C' class 0-6-0) and time in the signal box, etc. Interestingly even in the mid to late 1950s the station foreman and I used to walk the 'cripple' sidings counting the wagons awaiting repair into 'railway owned' or 'privately owned' groups! Happy Days."

It is with regret that we have been unable to find a view of Deal station and more especially the type of shunt described by Ray Grace – but we will keep looking. Meanwhile the first of two images of the LCGB special of 11 June 1961 mentioned by Peter Swift. This first shows 'H' 31308 and 'D1' 31749 leaving Tonbridge. *R C Riley/The Transport Treasury*

Now the return run recorded at Wadhurst, this time with 'L1' Nos 31749 and 31786 in charge. The staggered platform, here and at so many former SECR stations, shows up well. *R C Riley/The Transport Treasury*

Almost the view from Waterloo signal box and with a definite interloper in the ranks of a pannier tank engaged in carriage shunting. With the demise of the M7s on such duties, the GWR design filled a gap until their roles were taken over by the Ivatt and BR Standard tank types.

Now from **Peter Swift**. "With reference to the letter from Alastair Wilson published in **SW48** he enquired about **sightings of ex-SECR D1/E1 classes operating over the Tonbridge – Hastings line.** He mentions seeing a published photograph of E1 No 31507 at Wadhurst in 1958. I suspect this is the same photograph that has appeared in other publications in which case it was taken by Ken Wightman in June, though one caption suggests 1957 not 1958. Whichever year, it was towards the end of regular steam passenger workings over the Hastings line (this did bring the photographers out in force, thankfully). The only other photograph(s) I recall seeing covering the late SR and BR(S) period of D1/ E1 workings on the line was the LCGB special 'The South Eastern Limited' which ran on Sunday 11 June 1961. This train started from Victoria, making its way to Paddock Wood, via Strood and Maidstone West, for a final service over the Hawkhurst Branch, which closed that weekend, before making its way to Tonbridge. Here the train was taken over by 'D1' No 31749, piloted by 'H' class No 31308 to Robertsbridge. After a run over the K&ESR line to Tenterden and back (Terrier-hauled of course), the homeward run back to Charing Cross was double-headed by 'D1' No. 31749 but this time piloted by 'L1' No 31786. The train progressively lost time throughout the day and was photographed just over an hour behind schedule by Dick Riley mounting the summit at Wadhurst at 7.30pm that evening.

Returning to normal regular workings – when Alastair first observed the line in 1947, it was principally operated by locomotive duties shared between Bricklayers Arms, Tonbridge and St Leonards sheds. Taking Wadhurst as an observation location that year, one would have seen on a Mon-Fri four BA duties (1 x E, 1 x L1, 2 x V classes), nine TON duties (1 x C, 1 x H, 3 x L, 3 x N1, 1 x R1), nine STL duties (1 x C, 1 x D or L, 1 x L, 1 x L1 or V, 5 x V). Of these, four of the TON duties, plus one BA duty, terminated at Wadhurst and wouldn't have been seen at Robertsbridge. However, there they would have the benefit of a terminating St Leonards '01' class goods working. There was also one sole Hither Green shed working (Duty 183); this being an 'N1' class working the 7.05am Tonbridge to Battle goods (stopping off at Wadhurst between 7.53 to 8.35am) and returning on the 5.25pm Hastings – Hither Green goods. As can be seen, a potential of five 4-4-0 classes could be seen but not normally any 'D1' or 'E1' classes as none at this period was allocated to the depots in question. But we all realise that occasionally a shed foreman would either 'beg, borrow or steal' a locomotive from another shed to keep his rostered duties running, plus of course special workings,particularly during the summer months, so one can't be ruled out. By 1949 with locomotive re-allocations there was a greater chance of seeing a 'D1' /'E1' on the line, as by May that year there were three 'D1's allocated to Tonbridge and three 'E1's

Progress at Torrington with a quarter mile of track laid in the direction of Bideford. A great combination of preservation and a cycle way. (What better way could there be; exercise and trains combined!) *Rod Garner*

to Bricklayers Arms sheds. Even so, in subsequent years I have only seen the two photographs mentioned that have recorded either of these two classes working over the Hastings line, and like Alastair I also would like to hear of any other observations, or indeed other unusual locomotive workings, over the Tonbridge – Hastings line."

As a general enquiry, **Ross Shimmon** has been in touch reference the **Hayling Island branch**. We know this short line from Havant was the haunt of the 'Terriers' for many years but Ross asks if anyone has a view of a 'P' class tank on the line? We know that at least one of the class was based at Eastleigh for a short time – R C Riley recorded it at Winchester deputising for the more normal 'B4' shunter – but did it ever deputise for a 'Terrier' as well?

We now 'sit corrected' by **Neil Knowldon,** who correctly comments that the EMU near Sidcup on page 57 **SW49** is not a SUB, but an EPB.

Neil continues, "…Thanks for more fascinating insights into the Southern – which elicit a few comments: –

P54: Clipped round buffers and a turnbuckle underframe would date the Gresley Brake to about 1930 (so post-GNR). P56: If its got a Pullman rubbing plate and 'buckeye' coupling it's a 4-EPB. P58: I see TWO discs on No D5002 and this looks nothing like any Mid-Kent station I know … It'll be the Maidstone West line and a straight approach to a level crossing would suggest Beltring or Yalding looking south. P60: The Channel Island boat train may have only resulted in eight minor human injuries – but four carriages were burnt out: Maunsell First No 7227, 'Ironclad' Firsts Nos 7180 & 7169 and Pullman Buffet First "Rainbow". The three Southern chassis were recovered and used for Pull & Push Driving Trailers 6408/6/7 in 1937 using, as was usual for the Southern, stretched bodies from LSWR 50' Composites. "Rainbow" languished in store through the war years and emerged from Preston Park as Parlour First "Phoenix", styled to match the 1951 'U' type Cars (as exemplified by "Pegasus" on the rear cover). P65: "The Book of the M7 0-4-4Ts" advises that Nos 30039 & 30322 both entered Brighton on 27/3/57 and they left about a month later on 30/4/57 & 28/4/57 ; the Heavy Intermediate overhaul of the former only taking two days longer than the Light Casual of the latter. (By this time the 'R1's were virtually confined to the Folkestone Harbour Branch so – with Ashford in between – its unlikely any received attention at Brighton.) P69: Harry Wainwright obviously made a serious error when designing his locomotives, as he didn't add 2" high polished brass letters to the steam reversers stating what they were – thus leading to confusion among many generations of

Our final illustration is one from Ian Nolan which arrived as a result of our inclusion of the LNER type brake on an otherwise rake of SR stock on a through train. See P89, SW47. Ian asks if the vehicle could be a Pigeon Brake as per his own image of Gresley full brake Pigeon van No 4271 taken at Southampton on 26 April 1970 – he thinks the vehicle was labelled BGP – 'Brake Gangway Pigeon'.

railway journalists. Yes, the Westinghouse pump is a Westinghouse pump and the 'C' class one of the few so fitted: Nos 272 & 711-25."

Two more for this issue, the first from **Robin Thorne** re **SW47**. "Just to say how I enjoy each issue of Southern Way. The one including Waterloo Station Master was especially good for me as I worked as one of two Signal Lads in the box at Waterloo (six of us round the clock). I would like to just make a slight correction, as my memory from 1945-47tells me there were 309 levers not 307 ending on the Windsor line frame. There were two boys on each shift, one for the Windsor Signalman and one shared with the local and Main Line frames. Duties were round the clock including nights and a double shift eight hours, an eight hour break and then a second eight hour shift at weekends. All this for just 14 years of age and just so one boy could have a Sunday off. I can say it now but we were allowed to work the frame on Sundays. When time permitted, we would play shove-halfpenny on the floor with the regulator and the signalman.

The usual mistake with the frame was to pull off for the wrong platform outwards and need to scream out for the resident linesman to unlock the platform signal. We boys were also allowed to doze behind the frame on nights if we had

been out socialising all day, while the signalmen themselves did the booking."

Finally the human touch from **Ken Lawrence** on one image within **SW40 page 67**. "I am not a regular subscriber to SW (shame – Ed!) but having recently bought a copy of issue 40, imagine my surprise to find that I believe it features an image of my mother.

Marjorie Goodall was a typist with the Engineering Department in the offices above the concourse at Waterloo in the years leading up to WW2. These offices were then evacuated to Deepdene House near Dorking.

Ironically she was living at Merton Park during the War and had to commute back in a blacked-out train towards the bombing every night. I recall one story of the train coming to a halt near New Malden, and my mother and Mr A B McLeod (ex-head of IOW Locomotive, Carriage & Wagon dept and then Assistant Western Division Locomotive Running Superintendent) walking all the way back into London together.

My mother passed away this year, shortly before her 99th birthday, and those railway years were always remembered with great fondness."

Down to Earth Part 1

Mike King

This ex-South Eastern Railway brake van (or 'break' as the spelling would then have been) was built at Ashford Works in 1889, believed to be SER No 2483. It was allocated the SR number 55189 and Diagram 1552 at Grouping, but was never renumbered or repainted in SR brown livery – at least not to run in traffic. Instead, it was withdrawn in July 1928 and grounded at its place of birth – to be used as an office within the works, remaining there until the early 1970s. The writer saw it at Ashford and resolved to return to measure it up. This he attempted a couple of months later, only to find an empty space! Enquiries from local railwaymen elicited that the body had been sold to another employee and had moved to a garden "somewhere in Ashford". Measurement was therefore curtailed – or prevented – or so I thought. This was until about 1990 when the Kent & East Sussex Railway reported the acquisition of an old SER brake [brake – see image 040] van from Ashford. A visit to Tenterden soon after confirmed it was one and the same van, so it was duly measured and became Figure 52 in "An Illustrated History of Southern Wagons, Volume 3". This is the ancient body, temporarily mounted on a much more modern underframe, at Tenterden in the 1990s. The roughly planked section of bodywork at the nearer end marks the former position of the side lookout. The roof has clearly been covered with modern roofing felt. Regrettably, little or no restoration was carried out by its new owners and the van later moved to the Rother Valley Railway group at Robertsbridge station. However, a recent Google search of the Vintage Wagons Trust website has failed to find it, so the present situation is unknown. *Author*

With apologies to Monty Don, who has published a gardening book with the same title! However, here we are not going to pick up a garden fork or a rake, but instead look at something completely different; the various Southern carriages and wagons that were grounded or 'put out to grass' once their running days were over; for further use on the track side and at other locations as either storage, temporary office accommodation, cycle sheds, hen houses and, sometimes, even as homes for people to live in. There is, in fact, a very loose connection with gardening, as the SR allotments association was a great user of grounded ex-LBSCR goods vans – of which more later.

The uses and places to which old carriage and wagon bodies could be put were indeed many and varied – and over the years I, together with a number of other Southern rolling stock enthusiasts, attempted to compile a register of such vehicles. The number comes to well in excess of 1,200 vehicles and these are just the ones that I have come across – doubtless some readers will know instantly of one that is totally unknown

A slightly more typical grounded ex-SER van – albeit standing on trestles to facilitate unloading of wagons on the adjacent siding straight into the van body. Although also at Tenterden, but in independent railway days, this van did not survive into preservation. SER No 5339 dates from as far back as 1874 and became SR No 44688 to Diagram 1419 after the Grouping. It was withdrawn about 1930 and sold to the then independent Kent & East Sussex Railway, being grounded at Tenterden Town station, where it remained until at least closure to passengers in 1954. In this 1948 picture the former SECR World War One era lettering has reappeared, but pictures from an earlier period still show traces of SR lettering. Subsequent to this picture being taken, the body was repainted all-over green. *J L Smith*

to me and my gang of observers. Once upon a time, many stations and goods yards held the odd one or two, but other locations, such as the main workshops (ie, Eastleigh, Ashford, Brighton and Lancing) could boast whole collections of them – and it was sometimes a challenge to correctly identify them, especially if they had been rebuilt or hacked about – to make them suitable for their new roles. At certain coastal locations, particularly in Kent and Sussex, whole villages of such bodies once existed – but the march of affluence since the 1960s has severely depleted their numbers. Some of these were incorporated into larger structures or have disappeared behind home-made Gothic verandas and the like and may be difficult to identify as former railway vehicles. Yet, despite this, occasional carriage bodies do come on the market for sale, or are offered to the preservation societies as redevelopment of the sites take place.

It is perhaps not surprising that the railways used old stock for their own purposes. After all, they had an almost limitless supply of old vehicles from which to choose – they were soundly built and could give many more years of service on the ground when no longer fit to run in trains. The modern prefabricated and highly portable buildings that we take for granted today were just not available, and neither were there big road cranes available to lift them into position easily if located away from railway premises. So – up (or perhaps more accurately down) sprang grounded bodies. Track side examples probably began to appear as early as the 1850s, but by the late 19th century some began to be sold off to private individuals. The late Roger Kidner once wrote that the process of selling carriage bodies began with the Great Eastern Railway, who for the princely sum of £5 would deliver a body to suit your requirements to your local station. How you got it to site from that point was presumably up to you, and could involve horses and trailers, road lorries, barrels, timbers, jacks and a great deal of muscle power! By the end of World War One such sales became commonplace, while the increased requirement for temporary accommodation or dispersal during World War Two gave further impetus to the procedure.

An ex-LCDR van body, still displaying its SECR identity at Stoke Junction Halt on the Allhallows branch in April 1954. This was LCDR No 1538, which became SECR No 10186 after 1899 but was withdrawn about 1920 and grounded at this location prior to 1923. Had it survived into SR ownership, Diagram 1423 would have been allocated but some identical vans continued to run until about 1935. Clearly, no repainting took place before grounding and the van continued to show its SECR identity to the end. It was broken up about 1958. *J Berry*

Nowadays, few of these bodies exist. Many wayside stations have long since lost their goods yards, many other railway facilities have closed or been rationalised and the land adjacent sold off for redevelopment, while people demand better living accommodation than an old coach body – such have times changed. When I first began recording them, in the 1960s, a great number could still be seen – by then, however, they were often derelict, sometimes even starting to fall down, but most were still recognisable for what they once were. For those readers into model making, what better use for one's early kit built coach that is no longer considered worthy of a place on the layout – just a bit of cosmetic weathering and place along the track or in the corner of a farmer's field. It also gives the opportunity to model something ancient and otherwise out-of-period for the layout in question.

Enthusiasts before me had also started to record these structures – and I was able to benefit from their research and notes. The late Denis Cullum compiled a list of coaches "OW" – by which he meant "Off Wheels" – but whether this was his own term or an official one from the railway (he was a Southern Region employee) I do not know, but he was not the only person to use this abbreviation. The late Phil Coutanche did the same, as did Dick Riley. Dick also contributed a list compiled by the foreman painter at New Cross Gate workshops in the 1940s, where many of the vehicles were prepared for grounding. Not only did he note the vehicle number, but also its intended destination and the colour in which it was painted before dispatch – presumably either still on its own wheels or on a flat wagon (either four-wheeled, six-wheeled or bogie – whichever was most appropriate). Generally they were painted a light grey – or green if they were to be placed on a platform or within station limits. Goods vans were not always repainted and often "landed" in whatever previous traffic livery they last carried. Time and the elements

would gradually break the paint finish down to show whatever livery was underneath – including the former vehicle number – and of course this last was the "holy grail" when discovering such a body at some remote location. However, the foreman painter's list was often very useful for confirming details.

One other enthusiast I should mention here is Roger Silsbury of the Isle of Wight Steam Railway. Because of its geographical isolation, the Island collected more than its fair share of sold off grounded bodies from the three IOW companies and Roger has compiled a list of them. In recent years the Isle of Wight Railway has benefited from his research and been able to recover many of these bodies for eventual preservation, using in most cases, former SR utility van underframes (shortened where necessary) for the running gear. Many others still remain in the queue for restoration at Haven Street even now. The great majority of these were grounded away from railway property and whereas a certain logical approach could be applied to tracing vehicles on railway land, finding them in other locations is often a matter of pure luck. An entry in the carriage register such as "Sold to Mr Smith, Wimborne, June 1919" does not help much in finding the vehicle concerned, never mind whether it is still there. Sometimes a drive or walk in the countryside would result in the discovery of a van or coach body on a farm, often distant from the nearest railway line, and it is probable that a greater proportion of today's survivors are in this category.

Before going on to describe some examples in detail – a word of warning to anyone thinking of trooping all over the country or to the various heritage railways to inspect such bodies. Many are privately owned or on private land and the owners will not appreciate hordes of enthusiasts trespassing on their properties. Likewise an operational heritage railway has its inherent dangers, so always seek permission before going to inspect them. I got something of a surprise when I knocked on a farmer's door near Dymchurch many years ago asking to look

Another SECR goods brake van body, seen near the Royal Military Canal at Ham Street, on the edge of Romney Marsh, on 21 June 1948, still displaying SECR livery and lettering, although its former number cannot be traced. This would have become SR Diagram 1553 after the Grouping and was one of 210 vans built to this design between 1879 and 1903. A total of 163 became SR property and the last was withdrawn about 1943, although only a handful survived beyond 1935. The former guard's compartment was at the nearer end, served by a single door each side (where the timbers are largely missing), while the goods compartment was accessed via the double doors nearer the right-hand end. This grounded body was last seen by the writer circa 1970. *J L Smith*

closely at his chicken house. Instead of a look of incredulity, the farmer's wife nonchalantly told me that I was the third person who had asked that question since the beginning of the year!! The coach bodies turned out to be of Metropolitan and LCDR origin and both were later preserved by the Kent & East Sussex Railway, so I have no doubt it was volunteers from Tenterden that had made the earlier visits. Readers wishing to see the sort of work involved in restoring such bodies to revenue-earning condition are advised to visit one of the heritage railways who regularly conduct tours of their workshops to view the work in progress. The Bluebell Railway, Mid-Hants Railway, Isle of Wight Steam Railway and the KESR, to name but four, all have such facilities open on certain days of the year where it is likely that ex-Southern and pre-Grouping SR vehicles will be seen in various stages of renovation.

In this series we will start off with a look at various items of grounded goods stock. By their nature, most open-type goods wagons do not lend themselves to further use and I have only encountered a couple of locations where such wagon bodies have been employed as coal pens, for silage or for aggregate storage and the like. One was at Oxford, where a former private owner wagon (or rather three sides of it, plus the floor) was in use as a coal pen, while several ex-LBSCR open wagon bodies were once used for similar purposes at Littlehampton Wharf – alongside the River Arun. Both locations have long ago been redeveloped as industrial estates and any trace of the former railway installations have disappeared. Redundant tank wagons (invariably private-owner vehicles) have also been used for oil storage; usually surrounded by a low brick wall

bund to contain any spillage – but no railway-owned wagons have been recorded in such usage, although an old milk tank wagon could conceivably be used similarly as a water tank. Occasionally former cattle trucks have been used as stables on farms – this being particularly popular in Scotland – and one or two SR vehicles were so used – but I have never recorded one in the south. This leaves us with the various types of van – or covered goods wagon – to give them their correct railway title, plus goods brake vans. The former were extremely commonly grounded – being relatively small and easily transported – both on and off railway property, while the latter sometimes proved useful as self-contained office-cum-storage units. Containers could also be used – these had the advantage that they already had hooks incorporated for lifting purposes. In the 1950s Chessington Zoo (now the theme-park Chessington World of Adventure) purchased a number of containers as stables and one that was used for antelopes gradually exhibited the SR "Door To Door" advertising logo on the side facing the perimeter fence – as the more recently applied brown paint finish deteriorated. None of this was visible on the public side, as that was kept spruced up by the zoo's maintenance staff. When I worked for civil engineering contractor Sir Robert McAlpine, we employed piling contractor Cementation on one job and they arrived complete with several (admittedly ex-BR) containers in which much of their equipment was transported. These were quickly and easily craned from the lorries on to and off the site at the start and end of the works. The late Terry Gough once recorded a Southern Railway 12 ton van on the back of a lorry in Cardiff,

A rather less typical grounded body (well, almost – it is actually on brick piers but still has its 'W' irons in place) was SECR No 6246 – this still being legible on the solebar in this September 1961 picture. Built by The Metropolitan Railway Carriage & Wagon Company in 1878, it and three others were later purchased by the South Eastern Railway and numbered 6246-49. With one exception, all were scrapped by World War One, but No 6246 was withdrawn in March 1913 and became a goods warehouse at Brasted station on the Westerham branch two months later – so states the SECR wagon register at the National Archives, Kew. Remarkably, it remained there until the line closed in October 1961. It was totally unlike any other ex-SER goods van and was much more akin to ex-LBSCR designs. Indeed, the writer thought it a former Brighton van and for many years recorded it as such. In order to make it suitable for its 'static' duties, the former pairs of hinged opening doors were replaced by a sliding door at each side – the one on this side now being missing. If the photographer stood at this location today he would be in danger of being run over – the station site at Brasted is now almost obliterated by the M25 motorway. *Dr T Gough*

doing service as a mobile workman's hut. So, whether you model a goods yard, construction site, zoo or Cardiff Corporation vehicles there is scope for almost anything!

One thought that might cross the reader's mind at this point (well, apart from questioning the writer's sanity – this is, after all, a pretty obscure subject!!) is "did vehicles from other railway companies become grounded in the south of England?" – to which the answer is undoubtedly yes. Goods vans, in particular, wandered far and wide – even more so since nationalisation – so one could easily encounter an LNER van on a Surrey farm, or conversely a Southern van somewhere in Wales or Scotland. "Foreign" carriage stock was more uncommon but not unknown in the south either, while it was also possible to find occasional SR coach bodies in the Midlands or North, but this was rather more unusual. There was even a grounded coach body in a field near Tisbury that for some time evaded identity. It turned out to be of Lancashire & Yorkshire origin, while in Dorset one could come across the odd ex-Great Eastern or even a Cheshire Lines Committee coach. From time to time the writer is sent a picture of a coach or 'van body at so-and-so location and asked to identify it. Most turn out to have originated from the local

pre-Nationalisation company, but not always. For example, in recent times, a GWR coach was found near Ripley in Surrey, while a local Midland & South Western Junction railway composite was found north of Andover. Not far from me, a few years ago there were no less than 17 (mostly BR) 'van bodies in fields to the west of Littlehampton, serving as piggeries, and were, from time to time, dragged around the fields by tractor. At one point, they were all lined up in a row. Now, all are gone, having been burned on site.

The accompanying pictures show examples of grounded goods vehicles, together with, wherever possible, their histories. The next article will move to carriage stock – where, it must be admitted, far more variety may be found. Readers with the five books in the "Southern Wagons" series (published by OPC between 1983 and 2008) will be able to find out more about each type of wagon illustrated, as I will use SR diagram numbers for identification purposes. It will also be noted that several inspected by the writer were measured up and subsequently drawn for use in these publications. There was, after all, some method in my madness!

Part 2 in this series by Mike King will appear in issue 52 and will feature grounded ex-LSWR coach bodies.

Having mentioned ex-LBSCR vans, we will now look at these. At Woking down yard in the late 1960s is LBSCR van No 8206 – the number being visible high up on the left-hand side. This was to SR Diagram 1433 and one of over 400 to become SR property at Grouping, although in fact the other three LBSCR van diagrams were all much the same in general appearance. No 8206 dates from 1912, became SR No 46554 and was grounded at Woking in 1942 – remaining there until the late 1970s, being used for storage purposes. The only items to survive are the two wagon plates – both now privately preserved. As noted in the main text, the SR allotment association would request this type of van to be grounded alongside their plots whenever possible and examples could once be found on the track side at many locations – including near Andover Junction, Ascot, Aldershot, Bordon, Brockenhurst, Chichester, Dorchester, Earlswood, Fareham, Hastings, Portsmouth & Southsea, Staines, Templecombe, Topsham, Walton-on-Thames, Wool and Yeovil Junction, to name but a few. Many of these were grounded in the early years of World War Two – when the "Dig For Victory" scheme to promote home-grown food was at its height. *Dr T Gough*

At Redhill in 1960 is similar Diagram 1433 van LBSCR No 3638/ SR 46298, now clearly showing the position of the pre-Grouping lettering. It dates from 1914 and the original recorded cost was £70. In this instance it was a replacement for a similar Stroudley-era van dating from 1890, which, in terms of bodywork if not running gear, would have looked almost identical. It was grounded at Redhill during World War Two, possibly for use as storage for the wartime strategic control centre that was set up at the location at that time. By locating at an important junction not too far from London, it was less likely to be disrupted by enemy bombing raids. Several carriage bodies were also sited here, to provide the necessary office accommodation. Similar van LBSCR No 3674/SR46308 is just visible to the right. A colour picture of this van appears in my album "Southern Wagons in Colour" (Noodle Books, 2013). *G Bixley*

A Diagram 1436 van (the 10-ton version of Diagram 1433, which was rated at only 8 tons) still on its wheels, but on an isolated section of track, at Crabtree Sidings, near Belvedere, seen in 1957. It was still in the same position on 20 August 1974, and was photographed by the writer on that day – apart from summertime growth on the trees the two pictures are almost identical! Denis Cullum would have recorded this van as being "ON" – i e on wheels and a few vehicles did manage to get used in this manner – otherwise stationary and off the running lines, but still with full running gear in place. Formerly LBSCR No 3713, it became SR No 46773 as late as November 1929. Its recorded cost was £288 – contrasting sharply with the cost of van No 3638 just six years earlier – and giving some idea of First World War inflation. The van was transferred to service stock in October 1937 and renumbered as No1188s, for the use of the Signal & Telegraph department. It returned to traffic use and was No 46773 in January 1939, only to return to service stock as No 1704s just three years later, at which time the side windows were cut in. It was 'grounded' at Crabtree Sidings in 1949, remaining there until 1978, by which time very few ex-LBSCR wagons survived outside the Isle of Wight. Purchased by the Kent & East Sussex Railway, it moved to Tenterden, but little work was done before a further move to the Isle of Wight Steam Railway in 2002. Since then, it has been fully restored to Southern Railway livery and numbered "fictitiously" as SR 46923 and is now on exhibition at Haven Street. *HMRS*

Grounded ex-LBSCR goods brake vans were a rarity and this is the only one known to the writer. It also has a very interesting history. This is former Freshwater, Yarmouth & Newport Railway brake van No 13, seen in use as a boat store at St Helens Duver in 1990. It was built by the LBSCR in 1877; one of LBSCR numbers 136, 138 or 139. All three were sold to the Isle of Wight Central Railway in 1902, becoming their brake van numbers 1-3. It is believed this was No 1, as the other two were recorded as being rebuilt at Newport Works sometime around World War One. When the FYNR was formed, they came to an agreement that the IWCR would operate the line on their behalf. This somewhat shaky agreement fell apart in June 1913 and the Freshwater company resolved to run the railway themselves. For this they needed stock, so the IWCR sold them 30 wagons, one brake van and 12 coaches for the purpose. The coaches eventually became FYNR Nos 1-12, the brake van followed on as No 13. It was withdrawn on 20 March 1926, (probably without ever receiving its allocated SR number, which would have been 56038) and was grounded at St. Helens beach soon after. It was later sheeted over completely and painted red but finally fell apart in 2002. It is drawn as Figure 53 in "Southern Wagons Volume 2". *Author*

We now turn to ex-LSWR vehicles. By far the majority of those grounded were 18ft long, outside framed vans of which SR No 44142 is typical. To Diagram 1410, examples of this low-roofed design were grounded all over south and south-west England from the 1900s to the 1950s and doubtless some still survive in gardens and farmers' fields somewhere, even if none now remain on railway property. This van was formerly LSWR No 14174 and dates from 1912. It was grounded beneath Tothill Road Bridge at Plymouth Friary, probably about 1939 or later and was still there in July 1970, when photographed. The area suffered badly from German air raids and possibly the van was used to replace storage facilities destroyed in the blitz. Its siting beneath the road bridge would have afforded a little more protection. There is just one little mystery here; according to SR records van No 44142 was actually to Diagram 1409 – a high roofed van with 3-part doors (see next picture) – so were the records incorrect, or had the van swapped its identity with another at some point? Such things did happen and would only ever be spotted by a railway enthusiast! *H R Walters*

The later LSWR covered goods wagon design is represented by Diagram 1409 van No 42794, here showing post-1936 lettering at Eastleigh in November 1973. Built in 1914 as LSWR No 4196, it features in "Southern Wagons Volume 1" as Figure 16 and was, in fact, the very first drawing completed for this series of books – as far back as August 1980. The van was one of five similar bodies noted at this location several years earlier, but was the only one to survive past 1972 (in fact to about 1985). Interestingly, it is surrounded by 'Terrapin' contractors' huts being used by the firm stripping out the former Eastleigh Carriage & Wagon Works buildings prior to their being turned into an industrial complex. Such ranges of hutting – along with Portakabin and others – have largely seen the end of former railway grounded bodies. They are more versatile, lighter and are built to be craned on and off road vehicles at construction sites and other locations where temporary accommodation is needed. *Author*

Ex-LSWR goods brake vans were equally unusual subjects to be grounded. This is Diagram 1541 van No S54660 at Eastleigh Works in the early 1960s. The tail lamp appears somewhat superfluous! The van was used as an office and was once LSWR No 5703, completed at Nine Elms Works in 1888. It was renumbered and repainted in SR livery at Lancing on 13 October 1928 and was next noted at Eastleigh in June 1939 boarded "To work between Eastleigh Loco Depot & Eastleigh Running Sheds only" – quite possibly the coal stage pilot brake van. If this was its duty, then it was later replaced by similar van No S54938. By December 1956 the stencil had changed to "Loco Works Use" and it was grounded by 1962. Although by then almost 75 years old, it clearly had not travelled far during its later years. By the 1960s very few Diagram 1541 brake vans were still in use on the mainland, but examples remained in daily traffic on the Isle of Wight until 1967. *Dr T Gough*

Something rather more unusual – an LSWR former Diagram 1701 gunpowder van grounded at Woking up yard, seen in the mid-1960s. There were just 12 of these, built over the period 1904-1912, and they resembled the once extremely numerous GWR 'iron mink' vans in dimensions if not in every detail. SR numbers were 61201-12, but there has always been some confusion about the exact identity of this van. It was finally sold to the Kent & East Sussex Railway in 1979 and their records state it was formerly LSWR No 1401, which later became SR No 61206 and finally internal user van No 080407 at Brighton in 1954, moving to Woking in 1956. However, BR records state that internal user van No 080407 was previously LSWR No 1426/SR 61207, being withdrawn in 1955. However, these records may now be academic, as the van is no longer listed in KESR records, and may have been scrapped about 2012. Fortunately, sister-van No S61209 does survive at the Yeovil Steam Centre, having become a Scottish Region departmental vehicle in the 1950s. In the picture, the former LSWR lettering may be clearly seen. *Dr T Gough*

By the time ex-Southern Railway vans were being scrapped, grounding of such vehicles was becoming a thing of the past, so considering how common these once were, relatively few saw further use in this manner – and those that were could more often be found either away from the Southern or sold off for use on farms, etc. A slightly more unusual van is No S50738, seen adjacent to Skenfrith Castle (its walls may be seen behind), Monmouthshire, in 1984. This was a Diagram 1478 banana van, one of 200 built at Ashford in 1935, and was probably withdrawn in the early 1970s. Of interest is the fact that this van no longer has its underframe – being of steel construction this was clearly more valuable as scrap metal, so the body has been disposed of separately. The yellow spot marking indicates additional insulation fitted in 1961, when the previous internal steam-heating equipment was removed. Steam would be applied once the vans were loaded at Southampton Docks and would ensure that the contents ripened during the journey to market. Not only did it achieve this, but it also woke up the spiders that travelled with the cargo and these would greet the unloaders at Nine Elms, sometimes with an unwelcome surprise! The monument is now in the care of the National Trust and, perhaps not surprisingly, a Southern banana van did not feature high on the castle's assets and has longago been dispensed with! This view was taken from the adjacent B4521 road, which passes the castle site. *G H Kent*

A Diagram 1486 ventilated meat van body – grounded at Sittingbourne and seen on 20 August 1974. Built in 1931 as SR No 51208, it was withdrawn in May 1961 and became internal user van No081293, used by the Commercial Department at Crawley until June 1966, when it moved to Ashford and later to Sittingbourne, where it was then grounded in the goods yard. BR records mark it as "missing June 1973", giving some idea of its date of arrival at Sittingbourne. It was one of at least ten similar vans appropriated for storage purposes at various locations during 1961, giving an idea of when such traffic ebbed away from the railway network although refrigerated meat traffic in containers continued for rather longer. Some of these vans were transferred to ordinary goods traffic around this time, losing all except one of the end ventilators in the process. Sister-vehicle No S51284 was one of these and was seen by the writer grounded in the village of Ystradfellte in the Brecon Beacons in June 1975. Two more ordinary ex-SR ventilated goods van bodies were also seen in the vicinity at this time. *Author*

As noted in the text, containers were also grounded or sold off from the late 1950s onwards. This is SR Diagram 3026 4-ton container No BD1235S (the S suffix indicating that it was of Southern origin), possibly at Ashford in the late 1960s or early 1970s. It was probably finished in either crimson or BR bauxite livery. Built in 1945, it was one of 93 completed for the Southern, together with 14 for the LMS. A total of 83 were still in Southern Region stock in 1961, giving an indication of how long they continued to run.

Five Specials Ascend 'The Alps' Part 3
The Final Two Rail Tours

Les Price

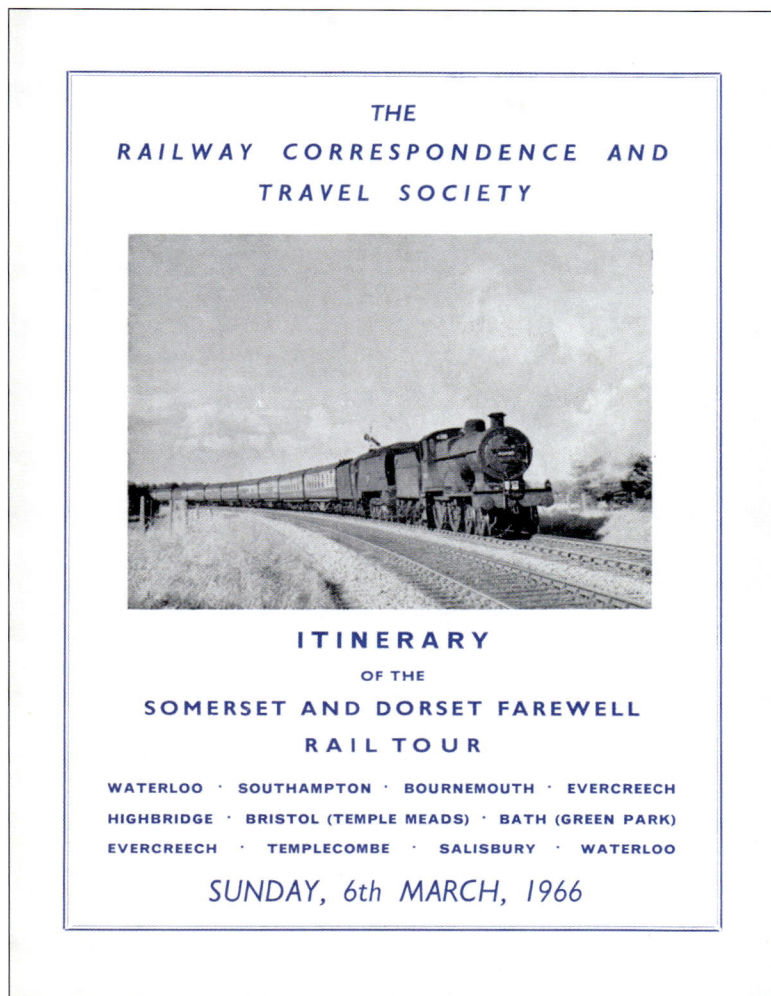

THE
RAILWAY CORRESPONDENCE AND TRAVEL SOCIETY

ITINERARY
OF THE
SOMERSET AND DORSET FAREWELL RAIL TOUR

WATERLOO · SOUTHAMPTON · BOURNEMOUTH · EVERCREECH
HIGHBRIDGE · BRISTOL (TEMPLE MEADS) · BATH (GREEN PARK)
EVERCREECH · TEMPLECOMBE · SALISBURY · WATERLOO

SUNDAY, 6th MARCH, 1966

Having recounted the exploits of the three 'Specials' over the Alps during the first quarter of 1966 we now come to the final two. The penultimate train also happened to coincide with the final day of operations over the 'Somerset and Dorset'. Happily I was aboard with my old mate Roger, in this instance going over the 'Alps' was more by accident than design. The original plan had been for the train to cruise down the LSWR main line from Waterloo to Southampton. But engineering works interfered with this and the train was therefore diverted from Pirbright Junction via Alton and so once again over 'The Alps' to Winchester.

'The Railway Correspondence and Travel Society' had organised 'The Somerset and Dorset Farewell Rail Tour' for Sunday 6 March 1966. The nine coach formation from Waterloo was in the charge of 'Merchant Navy' Pacific No 35028 *Clan Line*.

The original itinerary for the day showed the train running direct to Poole on the Southern main line but even from the start there was a diversion as we were routed via Richmond, Staines, and Virginia Water before re-joining the main line at Byfleet. Fortunately there was sufficient flexibility in the schedule to cater for this arrangement. Our steed, the trusty *Clan Line*, had also provided the power for the 'Dorset Belle' a week earlier. Even allowing for the additional mileage the schedule was still on the relaxed side; as a result of which No 35028 was able to take it in her stride.

SCHEDULE

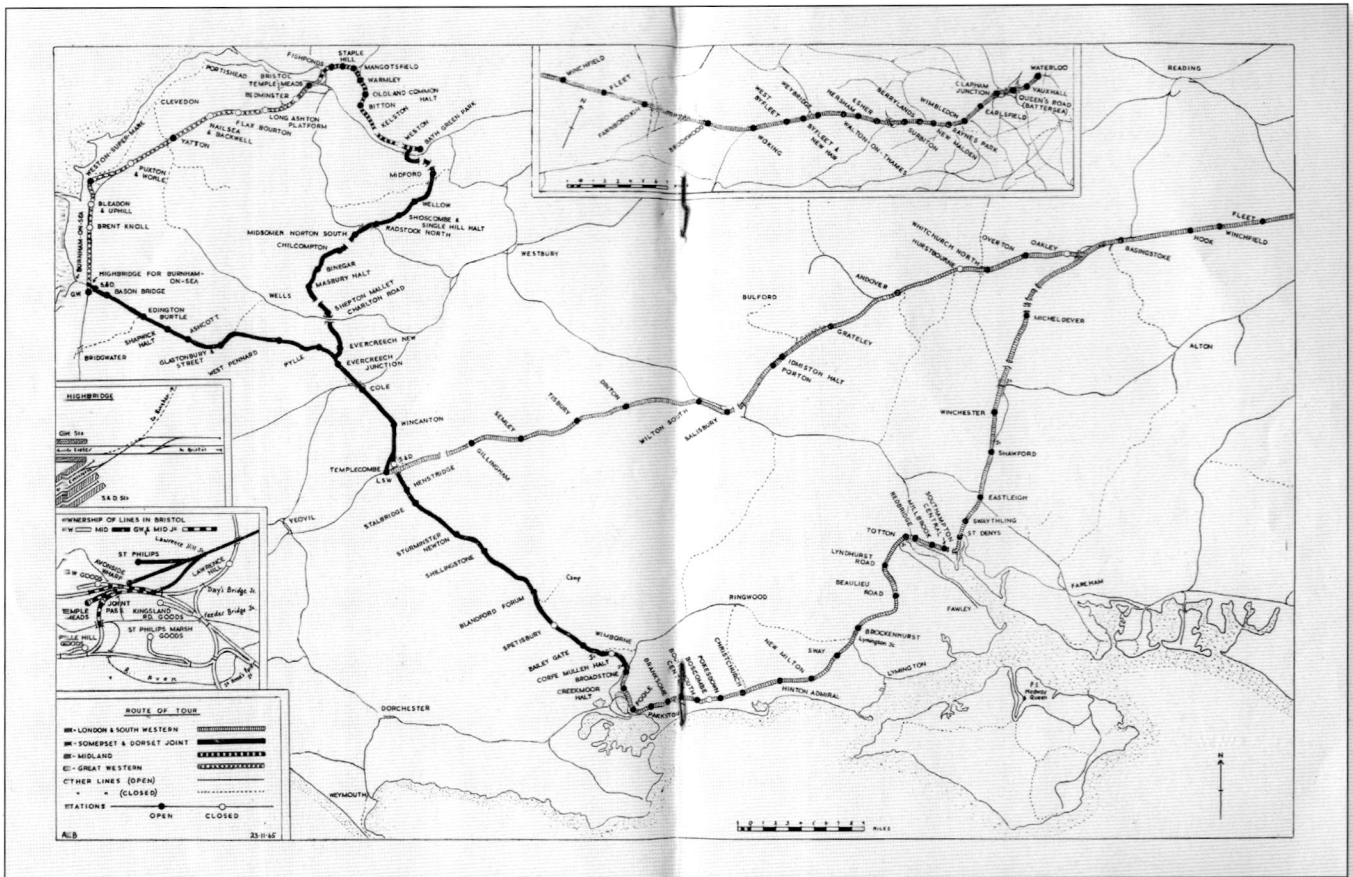

Mileage M. Ch.		Schedule		Actual
0.00	WATERLOO	dep.	09.00	
3.71	Clapham Jct.	pass	09.07	
11.20	Twickenham	"	09.22	
19.02	Staines Central	"	09.33	
23.16	Virginia Water	"	09.41	
28.02	Addlestone Jct.	"	09.50	
28.71	Byfleet Jct.	"	09.52	
32.30	Woking Jct.	"	09.56	
40.09	Ash Vale	"	10.09	
42.52	Aldershot	"	10.13	
54.37	Alton	"	10.29	
58.72	Medstead Home Signal	arr.	10.42	
		dep.	10.44	
64.47	Alresford	pass	10.55	
71.33	Winchester Jct.	"	11.07	
73.40	WINCHESTER CITY	arr.	11.10	
		dep.	11.15	
80.38	Eastleigh	pass	11.25	
86.12	SOUTHAMPTON CENTRAL	"	11.35	
100.53	Lymington Jct.	"	11.52	
114.75	BOURNEMOUTH CENTRAL	pass	12.16	
120.55	Poole	"	12.25	

Mileage M. Ch.		Schedule		Actual
124.09	BROADSTONE	arr.	12.32 P	
		dep.	12.42	
127.09	Corfe Mullen Box	pass	12.48	
135.00	BLANDFORD FORUM	arr.	12.58 W	
		dep.	13.08	
140.37	Shillingstone	pass	13.20	
143.40	Sturminster Newton	"	13.26	
147.38	Stalbridge	"	13.32	
151.11	TEMPLECOMBE JCT.	arr.	13.38	
		dep.	13.48	
161.31	EVERCREECH JCT.	arr.	14.07 WP	
		dep.	14.17	
172.08	GLASTONBURY	pass	14.50	
184.01	HIGHBRIDGE (S. & D.)	arr.	15.12	
	HIGHBRIDGE (G.W.R.)	dep.	15.35 K	
191.21	Uphill Jct.	pass	15.48	
192.72	Weston-super-Mare	"	15.51	
195.15	Worle Jct.	"	15.55	
211.79	BRISTOL (TEMPLE MEADS)	"	16.16	
217.06	Mangotsfield	"	16.29	
217.47	Mangotsfield North Jct.	arr.	16.31	
		dep.	16.41 CE	
227.58	BATH GREEN PARK	arr.	16.58	
		dep.	17.18 CE	
228.19	Bath Jct.	pass	17.20	
232.07	Midford	arr.	17.28	
		dep.	17.38 P	
238.30	Radstock North	pass	17.47	
244.63	Binegar	"	18.06	
249.29	Shepton Mallet	"	18.14	
254.12	EVERCREECH JCT.	"	18.23	
261.14	Wincanton	"	18.39	
264.65	TEMPLECOMBE	arr.	18.47	
		dep.	19.08 CE	
271.49	Gillingham	pass	19.16	
290.63	Wilton South	"	19.43	
293.16	SALISBURY	arr.	19.47	
		dep.	19.52	
326.57	Worting Jct.	pass	20.24	
329.17	BASINGSTOKE	arr.	20.28	
		dep.	20.30	
352.19	Woking Jct.	pass	20.58	
373.09	Clapham Jct.	"	21.18	
377.00	WATERLOO	arr.	21.25	

CE — Change engines
W — Water
P — Photographic stop
K — Passengers detrain and make own way to G.W. station whilst train shunts.
Motive power — Waterloo to Templecombe Jct. Merchant Navy Class
Templecombe Jct. to Highbridge Two LMS Cl.2 2-6-2T's
Highbridge to Mangotsfield N. Jct. Modified West Country Class
Mangotsfield N. Jct. to Bath Green Park Hymek Diesel
Bath Green Park to Templecombe Unmodified West Country Class
Templecombe to Waterloo Merchant Navy Class

Printed by Photomatic Limited, North Mymms, Herts.

Leaving Waterloo at 09:00 we had arrived at Alton by 10:25, fully four minutes ahead of schedule. Having taken the single line tablet, *Clan Line* then fairly stormed up the four mile climb at 1 in 60 to Medstead Home Signal in seven minutes against the scheduled thirteen. The result, of course, was that we then had to sit patiently awaiting the 09:53 Southampton Central – Alton, two car 'Hampshire' DMU which happily was running on time as indeed it had been the previous week for the 'S15' Rail Tour.

Leaving Medstead barely a minute late, we passed through Ropley, Alresford (exchanging tablets) and Itchen Abbas, and breezed back on to the main line at Winchester Junction without the delay experienced by the previous week's 'Special', so arriving at Winchester City almost five minutes early.

No 35028 paused at the extended platform at Winchester. (The extension was necessary to accommodate the future 12-car Bournemouth electric service.) Until the end of steam, water still needed to be provided, hence the water column sited at what had once been the limit of passenger access. The fireman can be seen bringing coal forward.

Here the engine took on water under the watchful gaze of a trainload of observers. We were due there at 11:10 and away at 11:15.

However, due to the enthusiasm of those on board we didn't get away until 11:17, two minutes late and shepherding them back onto the train wasn't easy! Thereafter we were treated to a stately ride through the New Forest, oblivious to trouble ahead.

A broken steam pipe meant we had to draw up at Branksome for remedial work to be undertaken. Coasting down the steep Parkstone bank almost to sea level at Poole we skirted Holes Bay, an inlet of Poole Harbour, forking north at Holes Bay Junction. Here the driver opened the regulator and *Clan Line* fairly galloped up the two miles at 1 in 75 through Creek Moor to Broadstone. Nevertheless, despite this effort, we were now twenty minutes behind time, due to the unscheduled stop.

It was a bleak March morning as a contingent of passengers warily stepped out of cosy carriages with windows obscured by condensation on to bitingly cold commodious platforms, intending to take pictures of a steam-enveloped 'Merchant Navy'. It was here, in former times, the Somerset and Dorset interchanged traffic with the 'Castleman's Corkscrew', the original route of the Southampton and Dorchester Railway; hence the spacious layout.

As with many of the Rail Tours of this period, again ushering passengers back onto the train at any photographic stop was not a simple process. The operators were fully aware there was a schedule to keep to; the passengers/enthusiasts totally oblivious! Unsurprisingly then, we were still fully twenty minutes late getting underway.

From here the train ran onto the first section of S&D single line as far as Corfe Mullen Junction where the original Dorset Central line came trailing in from Wimborne. A truncated part of this route remained until the section to Carter's Siding was closed in September 1959; this formerly served substantial clay workings. Thereafter, the rusting tracks down to our right remained *in situ* for wagon storage.

After closure to passenger traffic, Corfe Mullen Junction Signal Box still remained in service until 7 May 1968 when the siding was lifted. However, the route northwards to Blandford Forum remained open for freight traffic principally due to the milk factory at Bailey Gate. This was a United Dairies Cheese Factory with extensive sidings and one of the largest milk depots on the UK railway system; the tankers from here went to London. It lasted until 6 January 1969 when the remaining section of the S&D was finally closed.

Arriving at Blandford Forum at 13:30, there was a further booked stop for water. Meanwhile another Special had been travelling south over the S&D; the Stephenson Locomotive Society (Midland Area) 'Last Passenger Train on the Bath – Templecombe – Bournemouth Section'. This train had arrived at Blandford Forum on time, and had already waited 25 minutes for us.

Clan Line at Broadstone and the hardy few making their way back to the train after the stop here. The broken steam pipe issue had meant a late arrival at this stop.

Soon after our arrival it made a smart getaway, the fleetfooted amongst us able to photograph its departure. Stanier 8F No 48706, double heading BR Standard Class 4 Tank No 80043, made a fine sight as they strode out across the River Stour viaduct with safety valves blowing.

The 8F had been a Green Park (82F) allocated engine since June 1965, whilst No 80043 had been based at Templecombe (83G) since the autumn of 1964. Both locomotives were withdrawn on the closure of the S&D, so their round trip between Bath and Bournemouth was very probably their last duties. The Standard Tank had barely seen fourteen years' service, being released from Brighton Works in July 1952.

We left Blandford at 13:36 but there was little that *Clan Line* could do to regain time and we pulled up directly opposite the shed at Templecombe Junction at 14:00 again, still twenty-two minutes late. Here *Clan Line* was relieved and replaced by a pair of Ivatt Class 2 Tanks Nos 41283 and 41249, the lead engine being suitably adorned with a wreath displayed on its smokebox door.

A real effort had been made to present these engines in a fitting state. Each had polished smoke- boxes and No 41283, piloting, sported white painted buffers together with headlamp brackets supporting headlamps . Both engines were Templecombe-based and it is to the credit of the shed that its engines were being given a suitable send off. As with the locomotives on the SLS 'Special', the two tank engines were

also withdrawn after they had navigated the old S&D main line, followed by the Highbridge branch, for the last time.

We were the very last train to call at Evercreech Junction heading north, the station of course formerly one of the hubs of the Somerset and Dorset. An engine siding in the middle of the station was set between the 'up' and 'down' roads; it once held as many as five engines on a summer Saturday, having either come off or waiting to pilot heavy expresses over the Mendips.

There had also been an extensive goods yard here to handle exchange traffic but by now this had been largely lifted. This stop was shown in the itinerary as being for water and photographs but I do not recall any water being taken and in any event only ten minutes had been allowed for the stop.

A jaunty run across the Somerset Levels ensued from Glastonbury, following the course of the River Brue; spectators were out at each of the many isolated crossings, to see the last train go by. At Bason Bridge the single line squeezed its way past the narrow platform between the United Dairies milk factory on the north side and the River Brue on the other.

This factory (dating back to 1909) would continue to provide traffic to the section of line from here to Highbridge until 2 October 1972, when construction of the M5 motorway severed the link. During building of the new road this truncated spur was used to deliver 750,000 tons of fly ash to provide a firm base for the motorway across the Levels.

Nos 48706 and 80043 make a spirited get-away south from Blandford after being delayed pending our arrival.

The yard at Templecombe with withdrawn steam engines for which as at Bath (depicted later) there was no more work available. *Jeremy Staines*

The pair of Ivatt tanks, Nos 41283 as pilot and No 41249 as train engine, together took us down the branch and on to Highbridge. They are seen at Evercreech Junction with the appropriate wreath.

The train engine and with the driver perhaps impatient to get away.

Platform 5 at Highbridge S&D. The former company workshops may be glimpsed in the distance above the coaches. Here all passengers had to alight as they were not allowed to remain on board during the ensuing forward and backward shunt move.

The line then skirted the northern bank of the Brue all the way to Highbridge where we pulled into the grandly numbered Platform 5, the main S&D platform. By now the train had regained some time on a very accommodating schedule; we were only eight minutes late. Twenty-three minutes had been allowed to carry out the intricate manoeuvre from here into platform 6, the main Western Region 'Down' platform.

Initially the train had to cross the Western main line on the level to enter the 'Upside' Goods Yard. But first everyone had to de-train and by the time this had taken place, adding to the multitudes of local people, the station was absolutely crowded.

It has to be remembered that Highbridge, however small, was originally a railway town (once referred to as 'The Crewe of the West').Around 1862 the Somerset and Dorset built a Works here, fully equipped to maintain its own locomotives and rolling stock. At its height in the late 19th century it employed over four hundred people. Changing circumstances led to decline.

The works officially closed on 31 December 1929, making 300 men redundant in a town with a population of around 2,000. A few continued to be employed until the last jobs in hand were completed in March 1930. So the sight of the decaying ruins as we ran into Highbridge made a very sorry sight indeed. At the same time, this probably accounted for so many of the town's population turning out to witness the last rites on the line, with many among them quite likely descended from railway families. It was the final cut of the cord which had bound town and railway for just over a century.

To gain access to the Great Western main line the two Ivatts first gingerly drew their train past the former junction signal box and underneath the footbridge. Crossing the main line tracks on the level they rounded a very sharp curve into the Goods Shed. The clearance between the stock and the shed was a mere one and a third inches; hence the reason for detraining the passengers!

The tank engines were then put into reverse and slowly pushed the empty stock back into the main 'Down' platform where they left the train.

Meanwhile West Country Pacific No 34013 *Okehampton* had been waiting in the 'Down' Goods Loop. As soon as the two Ivatts had cleared, she had the 'tip' and cautiously nudged her way back through the swarming throng on to the front of the train. She too was extremely well presented; almost fit for Royal Train duty! No 34013 had been a Salisbury (73E) locomotive since September 1963. Was it there she was prepared for this duty or at one of the S&D sheds whilst in transit? Whoever it was had done a superb job.

The afternoon was creeping on as we left Highbridge at 15:41, six minutes down. With both junction signal boxes being switched out on the main line on a Sunday, we forked left at Uphill Junction to travel along the Weston-super-Mare loop before rejoining the main line at Worle Junction. After a sedate run through North Somerset and Temple Meads the train took to former Midland metals at Bristol East Box and arrived at Mangotsfield on schedule.

With the typical white embellishments of the period, No 34013 *Okehampton* reverses back on to the waiting train at Highbridge (WR) to head north to Bristol and then east to Bath.

Clearing the North Junction allowed a Hymek Diesel, D7014, to be attached to the rear of the train. We were now effectively topped and tailed. In this formation the Hymek led us to Bath (Green Park) with *Okehampton*' on the back, running in reverse. This north to south spur at Mangotsfield had not been used by a passenger train since the diversion of the 'Pines Express' in 1962. This line, along with the S&D, closed on and from 7 March 1966, which meant we were the last such train to use it – or did the SLS connection to the previously mentioned S&D 'Special' return north via this connection as well?

No 34057 *Biggin Hill* at Bath prior to the attachment of the second Bulleid.

Almost ready for the 'off' from Bath and the final passenger train south on the S&D. The siding containing the wagons originated near the shed entrance before turning through 90° as seen. There was also a throw-back to the goods shed.

At Bath Green Park *Okehampton* was detached to allow original 'Battle of Britain' Pacific No 34057 '*Biggin Hill*' to back on to the train prior to '*Okehampton*' rejoining as the pilot engine for the final trip over the Mendips. '*Biggin Hill*' was also a Salisbury engine, upon which an equal amount of cleaning had been carried out. So after arriving three minutes early we set forth slightly late at 17:27.

From taking the single line token at Bath Junction, 41 chains from Green Park, the line climbed for two miles on an almost unremitting ruling gradient of 1 in 50 to the mouth of Combe Down Tunnel.

The pair set about their task admirably and kept to schedule arriving at Midford four miles on, ten minutes later. A photographic stop was arranged here and with the sun setting at 17:58 the light was fading fast for photographers; it was the last opportunity. With the safety valves of both engines blowing hard, they clearly still had steam to spare; but the stiffest of the climb was yet to come.

Midford station was prettily situated on the side of a valley through which ran the Midford Brook, a small tributary of the Somerset Avon. Along this small valley also ran the Camerton branch of the former Bristol and North Somerset Railway, a branch line of the GWR. Its claim to fame comes as a result of the 1953 film 'The Titfield Thunderbolt', made on the last section of that line after it had been finally closed to all traffic on 15 February

1951. This film may arguably be considered as the spur to the sprouting of the whole railway preservation movement.

At Midford the line became double track, so the crew had already handed in the token from Bath Junction, when at 17:46, eight minutes late, we set out once more. Before us was the formidable climb to Masbury. Unfortunately our engines would not be allowed to have a fair crack at it due to engineering works consistent with the pending closure and consequently single line working was in operation between Writhlington Colliery sidings and Midsomer Norton but no allowance for this would seem to have been built into the schedule.

A new connection was under construction about a quarter of a mile west of the old S&D Radstock station. It was probably understandable that such work was being carried out on the last day of running since no operational staff would be available the following day. Nevertheless it had added to the complications of accommodating the final two 'Special' trains.

These works were due to alterations in respect of diverting coal traffic out of Lower Writhlington Colliery after the closure of the S&D. Initially this diversion allowed the surviving coal trains to be routed out via the old GWR North Somerset line to Bristol. After closure of its northern section, the remaining coal traffic was diverted via Frome. Subsequently Writhlington was the last colliery to close in the Somerset coalfield on 28 September 1973.

Redundant steam at Bath depot. Engines that might even have been good for service for a while longer but now, with no work for them here or elsewhere, there was nothing left but scrap.

After picking up our pilot man we left Radstock North at 18:08, 21 minutes behind time. Arriving at Midsomer Norton, we once again ran on to double track and here the returning SLS Special, itself now running an hour late, was waiting for us. Our two Light Pacifics now faced the final four mile climb to Masbury Summit, 811 feet above sea level. This was the toughest part of the entire climb over the Mendips, most of it being at 1 in 50 and similar to the climb out of Bath. Even so, despite a very slow start, the two engines tackled the climb with alacrity.

We swung through Evercreech Junction at 18:47, having lost only a further two minutes on the schedule. At Templecombe the train ran through on to the South-Western main line, enabling *Clan Line* to rejoin on the rear before leading the charge back to Waterloo. We left at 19:18, now only ten minutes down, whilst later by the time a crew change had been effected on the footplate at Salisbury this had been even further reduced.

From Salisbury a schedule of 93 minutes for the 84 miles to Waterloo had been set; not the glory of former days. But *Clan Line* and her crew rose to the challenge. By Woking, the deficit had been cut to two minutes; expectations rose. Alas signal checks as a result of on-going engineering works at Wimbledon once again hampered our progress and we finally arrived at Waterloo twelve minutes late at 21:37.

This had been an exceptional tour; if not unique. Unique in the sense that two major climbs had been included, namely over 'The Alps' and then 'The Mendips', all in the same trip with history having been made as well as previous historical events noted. Along with the other S&D stations, Templecombe was

also closed after our departure. By the time I revisited the town (in the early 1980s), it had been re-opened due to pressure from the local community and with the encouragement of Gerald Daniels, the Area Manager at Salisbury. Now the mechanical signal box also doubled as the ticket office!

We should note that in early 1966 steam on the Southern Region had less than 18 months left in operation and consequently on tours such as this, scheduling was no longer based on what might reasonably challenge the engine and its crew; rather than, given the lack of maintenance and general attention to locomotives, what may reasonably be expected, in order to accommodate the then current timetables. It is in this context that this train's locomotive performance should be judged.

The final special over 'The Alps'

We now come to the final steam 'Special' in 1966, which ran over 'The Alps'. Regrettably at the time, and due to a slender salary, my budget for rail tours was limited. As a result I did not travel on the LCGB 'Wilts and Hants Rail Tour' of 3 April 1966; nor do I have access to its itinerary.

However, the thing that was different about this tour was that it ran over 'The Alps' in the reverse direction on its return journey to Waterloo. The train had set out from London loaded to ten coaches behind Maunsell 'U' Class 2-6-0 No 31639, together with another Maunsell 2-6-0, 'N' class No 31411; both Guildford-based locomotives at the time. It is probably true to say that by this stage, Guildford had become the final home for the remaining pre-war Southern Railway engines.

In former years the 'U's' were known colloquially as 'U Boats', after the German s submarines during the First World War were matched with the 'U's' availability to operate almost anywhere throughout the Southern system. By contrast the 'N's were known as 'Montgolipers'; some connection to Montgolfier balloons perhaps? (If anyone can explain, it would be extremely useful!) Equally they were also known as 'Woolworths', as a consequence of fifty of the class being built from kits made at Royal Arsenal, Woolwich.

Clearly these engines had been kept in good operational condition to celebrate the last fling of steam. Both had appeared some months earlier on the LCGB 'Wealdsman' Rail tour on 13 June 1965 and then latterly with the 'S15 Commemorative' Rail Tour' previously mentioned. Double-heading together, on this train, they left Waterloo at 9:15am. *(The 'Wealdsman' tour will feature in a later issue of SW – Ed.)*

The tour ran out through the south London suburbs via Longhedge Junction and Norwood Junction to Redhill before, after a very convoluted route, arriving at Guildford at 11:54. Unlike the S&D tour described earlier, this train appears to have been running to schedule. A photographic and water stop was arranged here. It then ran across to Reading before returning to the Southern by way of Mortimer and Bramley to Basingstoke, there making another photographic stop.

Continuing on to Salisbury, the 'N' completed its journey.

After a 2½ hour break, the 'U' reappeared with 'Q1' 0-6-0 No 33006, which acted as train engine, and the 'U' as pilot. The 'Charlie' had been officially withdrawn from Guildford some three months earlier but like the 'S15', in Part 1 of this series, was shipped out for special occasions. It had previously been used on the LCGB 'New Forester Rail Tour' on 19 March 1966.

The train was due to leave Salisbury at 16:07 and ran pretty much to time, making ten minute stops at Romsey (for photographs) and Southampton Central, probably for water. The pair set out on schedule at 17:08 for the 1 in 252 climb from just beyond Eastleigh up to Winchester Junction to face 'The Alps' from the opposite direction. They must have made good time including the five mile climb from Alresford with a ruling gradient of 1 in 60 to the summit 652 feet above the sea at track level. They arrived at Medstead home signal four minutes early at 17:56.

Here the train waited for the Sunday 17:53 Alton to Southampton Central 'Thumper' due at Medstead at 18:02, that happily was running on time. From there it was all downhill, so to speak, and the train arrived at Waterloo fully nine minutes early at 19:18.

It has to be said that at the time of this 'Special', a great deal of ordinary passenger traffic was being diverted over 'The Alps' on Sundays because of the electrification of the main line from Waterloo to Bournemouth, hence it could have been difficult at times to find a spare path over the Winchester Junction to Alton single line.

We could not locate a view of the 31639/31411 Class 'U'/'N' combination of 3 April 1966, so instead we have this view of a pair of 'U' Class 'Moguls' Nos 31791 and 31639 on the 30 April 1966 RCTS (London Branch) Longmoor Rail Tour. The combination is waiting to depart from Waterloo just before 10.00am. *Jeremy Staines*

The public approach to Esher station, Up side, circa late 1950s. Note the shoe repair shed on the right-hand side. *The Transport Treasury*

This aside, the conclusion asks more questions than provides answers. Was this, indeed, the last steam special over 'The Alps'? Was it also the last such train headed by purely ex-Southern Railway built locomotives? Finally was it unique, in the last days of steam; was it the last steam special on the Southern to be double-headed? (Les asks the question and we can respond thanks to the excellent 'Six Bells Junction' website.) On 16 April 1966, Nos 31411 and 31639 were involved on the RCTS Longmoor Railtour, repeated with a similar combination, Nos 31791 and 31411, to the same destination on 30 April. (A double headed tour with either 34002 *Salisbury* or 34100 *Appledore* attached to 45393 ('Black 5MT' 4-6-0) operated on the lines between Waterloo, Salisbury, Yeovil and Weymouth on 3 July 1966.) We should also not forget the LCGB IOW tour of 31 December 1966, when W24 *Calbourne* and W31 *Chale* double-headed each way between Ryde and Shanklin. In addition, a planned tour involving double-headed Ivatt tank engines and double headed USA tanks over the Gosport, Fawley and Lymington branches was proposed for 24 September 1966 but did not run. Moving in to 1967, on 9 April the LCGB had double headed USA tanks over the Fawley branch, which lead to two tours in June 1967. The first was on 3 June 1967 operating as the 'Dorset Limited' which saw Nos 34034 *Honiton* and 35030 *Elder Dempster Lines* doubleheading on the section from Weymouth to Bournemouth. The second was on 18 June with 73029 and 34023 *Blackmore Vale*, and then 34023 and 34108 *Wincanton* on various sections of the RCTS 'Farewell to Southern Steam' event. Lastly was the BR 'Farewell to Southern Steam' tour of 2 July when 35007 *Aberdeen Commonwealth* and 35008 *Orient Line* double-headed between Weymouth and Bournemouth Central as part of the itinerary. (It is not believed there were any other special steam workings over 'The Alps' – Ed.)

Unless stated otherwise, all images are by the Author.

Now You See It – Now You Don't!
The Slotted Post Signal at Esher

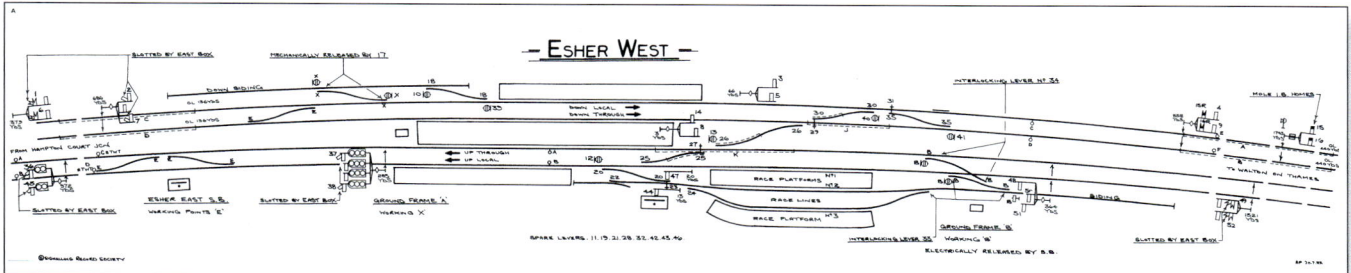

(Or what started off as a single article on just one signal and which just grew and grew...!)

In the early days of railways the first signals were those given to the driver by hand from a 'Policeman' at the side of the track. This then changed to a flag being held and then to a fixed disc or crossbar. After this came the semaphore type signal usually operated from a lever at the bottom of the post but which quickly altered to be operated remotely from a lever placed with others at a convenient location. Hence the literal meaning of the term 'signal box'. So much for a very general history of signalling, after which we turn to the actual signals themselves.

Railway signal design has naturally developed over the years with the earliest signals supplied to the various railway companies by one or more of the outside railway signalling companies. Over time the LSWR came to prefer the products of Messrs Stevens and Sykes, whilst in SR days the name of Westinghouse may be added. 'Relics' from the earliest days naturally began to disappear as the system expanded and was modernised and this included the original fixed signals; as an aside it would also be interesting to find out when the last 'disc and crossbar' type was removed from anywhere on the LSWR or other constituents of the Southern, certainly pre-grouping and likely pre-1900.

But some relics had a far longer life and the starting signal for up trains off Platform 1, one of the racecourse platforms

at Esher, would certainly fit that criteria. To explain, we first need to describe Esher itself. Originally part of the double track LSWR main line between Surbiton and Woking, quadrupling of the route had reached Surbiton in the east in 1884 but it took a further 20 years before the section on to Woking was fully quadrupled in 1904. Before the former date, a loop on the Woking side of the station at Esher, off what would later be the up local line, had been provided. This was immediately west of the main platform of what would later be the up slow line. This loop then split into two lines. On the north side was a single platform face, whilst between the up slow line and the south side of the loop was an island platform. Three platform faces were thus available. Joe Brown, in his excellent "London Railway Atlas 4th edition" (Ian Allan 2015), has the date for these as 20 April 1882. The whole being provided in connection with race traffic.

Turning now to the (post-1959) signalling diagram, we see the platforms numbered as 'Race Platforms 1-3', obviously accessed by up trains only. Actual services that might have used the facilities are unknown but the one thing that does seem slightly strange is that it would have been presumed that most racegoers to the adjacent Sandown Park course (opened in 1875) would have arrived from London in the down direction and where there was no separate platform dedicated just for this traffic. Possibly the operating arrangements were such that a special service in the down direction might disgorge its passengers before crossing over to the separate racecourse platforms away from the main line, here to await the return journey, or to wait on the up local line as described at the end of this piece. (I was very tempted to say '....to be stabled....' at this point!)

The face of the island platform alongside the main line, Platform 1, was likely used as a brief pause for racegoers and loaded special trains in the up direction although any such services would certainly not have been held here for long periods as this would otherwise occupy the up slow line – again see later notes.

Signalling diagram for Esher – pre-1959. Prior to July of that year there had been two signal boxes at the location, one at each end of the station. As was LSWR practice, the box nearest to London was 'East' and furthest away 'West'. At Esher this coincided with the points of the compass but it was not always the case elsewhere. (At Eastleigh, for example, where the railway runs almost 'north – south', 'East' box was on the north side of the station...) Returning to Esher, 'East' was closed from 5 July 1959 with all operations now under the control of the former 'West' box, (now simply renamed 'Esher') and conveniently located between the end of the Up local platform and the racecourse platforms. On the Down side a single siding will be noted at the London end of the station although in LSWR days three sidings are shown in the same position. *Signalling Record Society*

In the earliest days, slotted post signals could display one of three separate meanings but with just a single red or green light displayed at night. With the arm horizontal, painted red (was a white vertical band displayed as per later practice?), the meaning was 'stop' and the spectacle plate displayed a red light at night. 'Caution' saw the arm fall to 45° and now with the green light displayed. 'All clear' had the arm hidden in the post and again with the green light. The risks associated with this type of (mixed) indication are obvious and yet this type of signal was used on other systems elsewhere, the North Eastern Railway for example. Beyond the signal at the main station, the island platform facing the through lines is still present; the island platforms here, as well as those at Walton on Thames, Woking and elsewhere west as far as Hook were all later taken out of use. Note to the gate and what was a subway leading off the end of the island platform, this led to the racecourse. A slope to and then a subway, part of which is just visible in the foreground, also led from the racecourse platforms. Finally the railings surrounding the walkway on the outside of the operating floor of the signal box may just be seen on the left. This is a later image as a white 'track circuit' diagram is attached to the post of No 47 – see subsequent image as well.

The west end of Esher West signal box and an image that raises more questions. The view depicts what is shown as signal No 44 on the diagram and which, if we read it literally, applies just to Platform 3 – trains departing routed either to the Up local or Up through lines – except there is no crossover to the Up through line post-1959 at least until reaching Esher East at the London end of the station and where there is already a signal for that move! This would then explain facing point lock No 23 so indicating platforms 2 and 3 were used for passenger departures. On the 1959 diagram just a single arm is shown on the diagram, No 44 indicating the lower arm had been removed. This is a conventional Stevens type lattice signal post with lower quadrant arms. So far so good but what about departures from platform 2? We have no definite explanation on that point. It cannot be that No 47 applied to platform 2 as in the next view an EMU is seen arriving at Esher station passing No 47 in the 'off' position. There is absolutely no way No 47 could have applied to both the Up local and Platform 2 as it would otherwise have permitted a conflicting movement. So we ask again, what was the controlling signal allowing a train to exit from platform 2 and the answer is we just do not know. To confuse matters even more, on the reverse of the print the photographer has written "Signal at Esher West, controls exit from sidings to Up main lines'. *R F Roberts/Stephenson Locomotive Society*

The signal in use with an EMU passing. By this time the 45° angle for the arm meant 'off', the earlier caution display having been superseded by separate yellow painted arm distant signals. (The distant signals at Esher were repainted from red to yellow in 1927.) This view probably dates from a day when the platform would have been required to be used, with station staff and the local S&T fitter perhaps instructed to bring the signal into use ready for services later in the day. On such occasions the drivers of ordinary trains would comply with either of its two indications 'off' (as here) or 'on' (with the arm horizontal) as they would with any other signal. On the opposite 'Down' lines, is a standard SR tall bracket with arms for the 'Down through' line and 'Down through to Down local' line arms. (Respectively Nos 8 and 14 on the diagram, the latter via crossover 30. For the purpose of this text the numbers of facing point locks are not mentioned unless relevant to the narrative.)

By 1959 two separate starting signals were provided for trains leaving race platforms 1 and 2/3, that for Nos 2 and 3 is shown as a single arm, which would appear strange in itself having just a stop (proceed) signal to control the exit from two separate platforms. Presumably the Board of Trade would have approved the arrangement at some stage? The entry to racecourse platforms 2 and 3 was similarly controlled by just a single signal, No 51. It may also be noted that there is no facing point lock for the turnout, affording entry to Nos 2/3 once off the main line. This would therefore tend to confirm that the platforms were used more for horse box or passenger departures rather than passenger arrivals OR platforms 2/3 were used solely for stabling horse boxes which would be an alternative explanation as to why there was no facing point lock on the approach.

The signal controlling the exit for trains off platform 3 at least was a conventional semaphore, but the other signal for Platform 1, and the subject of this brief appraisal, was a slotted post signal that retained its slotted arm, we believe, until the race platforms were finally taken out of use in October 1965. (It may be not all the platforms survived in use until that final date.)

Operationally we now need to refer to the signalling diagram again. Notice the position of the signal in question, No 47 on the diagram and which might well be described as the 'up inner local home signal'. In theory at least. Should a train call at the 'Race Platform No 1', it could be held here to allow an overtaking train to enter the up local platform from the up through line by means of facing crossover No 25. But there would most certainly have been some very carefully worded instructions for this to take place as there is absolutely no allowance for safely (a 440yd clearing point) beyond No 47 and the trailing end of crossover No 25! Possibly if this type of move was necessary the signalman would first have to satisfy himself the train at 'Race Platform No 1' was indeed stationary at No 47, before he was allowed to alter the position of crossover No 25 and only then lower the 'up through to up Local home signal' (No 50) on the bracket 364 yards from the signal box. This could also only have applied in clear visibility and certainly not in 'fog or falling snow'.

Finally, we might add that in attempting to understand the workings of the racecourse platforms at Esher, we have consulted as many sources as possible. This includes the various Sectional Appendices, which, whilst not mentioning the signal in question, do refer to the practice of stabling empty trains (clearly out of peak times) on race days, along the up local line between Walton and Esher – akin to 'permissible block' working.

We now see the same signal (No 47), this time with the arm hidden within the post – drivers would regard this as meaning 'off'. When not in use, a pin would be inserted through the post and arm to ensure the arm remained hidden; the hole for this may be seen in the various views.

A close up of the signal very clearly at 'on'. Perhaps an occasion when there were stabled trains nose to tail in line on the Up local?

Probably an S & T fitter, perhaps attending to a defect or maybe attempting to move the arm from one position to the other – with other helpers 'watching'! Likely summer time as the man is just in shirtsleeves whilst the actual post has also had a repaint at some stage. Track circuit 'diamond' more plainly visible. (This meant that if the driver of a train were held at this signal, he had no need to visit the signal box to carry out 'Rule 55'; reminding the signalman of his presence and staying in the signal box long enough to see a 'reminder collar' was placed on the signal to the rear. This was because the track circuit would electrically [electronically ?] advise the signalman in the same way.) It is likely the signal was removed as being of no further consequence around the time the racecourse platforms were abandoned; therefore its historic significance is lost. At least one other slotted post, but not a slotted arm, remained in use until the 1960s on the Andover to Romsey line between Horsebridge and Mottisfont. Here the signal arm had been refitted on the outside of the post, thus meaning the slot was no longer in use. We would be interested to learn of any other SR examples that survived into the 1960s.

The slotted post between Horsebridge and Mottisfont but with the arm remounted on to the facing side of the post.

The full instructions are reproduced below and are taken from the Southern Railway Appendix to the Working Timetable dated 26 March 1934 'until further notice' and with similar, if not identical, instructions certainly in force by the LSWR in 1911.

"Between Esher and Walton. Berthing empty trains on up local line. Between certain times on Sandown Park race days, as advised by special notice, empty trains will be berthed in close order on the up local line between Walton station up local starting signal and Esher West up local home signal, when the following arrangements will apply.

"After the Train out of section signal for the last train allowed to proceed on the up local line before that line is used for berthing empty race trains has been received at Walton and the block indicator applicable to the up local line is in its normal (line blocked) position, the Signalman must make an entry in the Train Register Book, viz, up Local Line Blocked, and place a lever collar on the lever of the starting signal applicable to the up local line. The Station Master, after seeing that arrangements for blocking the up local line are complete and satisfactory, must advise the Inspector in charge at Esher by telephone, and thereafter empty trains may be marshalled in close order on that line under the supervision of the person in charge of empty train working.

"Drivers may pass the Walton up local starting and advanced starting signals and Mole* Intermediate up local line home signals at Danger when so instructed by the person in charge of the empty train working. When the return traffic commences, empty trains will be worked forward as required, and after the first train moves away from Esher West box up local home signal, succeeding trains must move along keeping their close formation, but must not proceed beyond that signal until verbally instructed to do so.

"The person in charge of the empty train working at Walton must travel with the last train to be run in close order on the up local line, and he must advise the Signalman at Esher West when the up local line from Walton to Esher West is clear. He must similarly advise the Signalman at Walton by telephone, and the latter must make an entry in the Train Register Book, viz up Local line Clear, after which normal working on the up local line may be resumed, the Driver of the first train to pass through the sections to Esher West being instructed to proceed cautiously.

"Should the last empty train be unable to run to the home signal at Esher West when the line is clear for it to do so, or in the event of the last empty train being unable from any cause to follow up the previous train in due course, the Guard must protect it in accordance with Rule 179."

The Mole intermediate signals replaced the former signal box at Mole, located on the north side of the line 1m 10ch west of Esher West signal box. Mole had been closed as a signal box in 1932.

To complete the sequence, we have an interior view of the interior of Esher West signal box with Signalman Skelton, 2 April 1953.
R F Roberts/Stephenson Locomotive Society

Air smoothed...?

We were recently afforded access to another new collection of colour slides, always welcome of course and containing the usual eccentric mix, the reason for which is probably only known to the original photographer. It was whilst rummaging through these and viewing same on the lightbox that an idea began to gel as first one then two and finally five separate images emerged with the same theme – the 'air-smoothed' casing of the original Bulleid design.

Now before going further, let me say I have not set out to criticise anything at all, merely to display an aspect of the design, which may not have been seen as a whole when compared with other members of the class.

Now back in 1945 and through to 1950, when the engines were emerging from Brighton and Eastleigh, it is probably fair to say that no two were exactly the same. True they were built using the same drawings and whilst nowadays we have computers to design and robots to assemble machines whereas back then it was recourse to the drawings, which were translated by men and who in turn then produced the actual component – and a grand job they did as well.

Come the final part of the Bulleid design though and perhaps different thickness metals were used for the exterior casing whilst in addition wear and tear in service could ripple, twist and generally distort thin metal sheet and of which basically all the casings were made . Mr Bulleid had designed engines, the exterior of which had an 'air-smooth' exterior – being careful to note not streamlined. He had intended these to go through the equivalent of a carriage washer but no such equipment was ever provided, though one may indeed have unintentionally – and probably against all the rules – ventured through a carriage washer, this would only have been when pushing or pulling a rake of coaches. What effect any such move might have had on the sides of the locomotive is not recorded. (Probably 'not a lot' for a carriage was basically a vertical side whilst the engine design tapered inwards.)

Some engines too appear to have had a better casing than others, whilst so far as the accompanying images are concerned, we should mention that the actual casings used, the cleanliness (or otherwise) of the engine, the angle of the photograph and especially the lighting could all make a difference. Even so we hope you enjoy this small selection.

No 34103 *Calstock* generally good but elsewhere clearly a broken slide to the sand box.

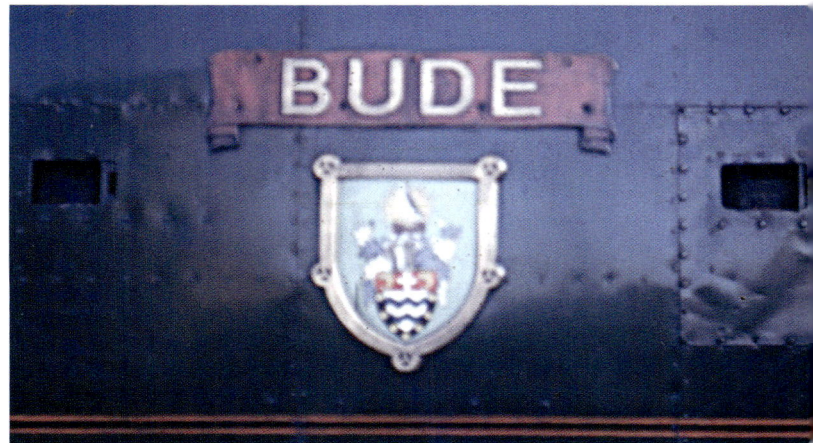

No 34006 *Bude,* similar and in mostly reasonable condition, apart that is from the replacement casing around the rear sandbox, a modification perhaps requiring the original to be cut away?

No 34019 *Bideford.* Not perhaps the best lighting but generally living up to the 'air smoothed' name; underneath all that grime that is!

Oh dear, No 34057 looking almost like a creased photograph (the slide was most definitely NOT creased). Neither have we attempted to manipulate any of the images to obtain the results currently desired."

And the ultimate, but perhaps not something to be especially proud of No 34015 Exmouth, perhaps not helped by the side lighting. Was it and the others really as bad as this appears to be or is this indeed an example of poor fitting in the first place? The whole thing really does look like a piece of crinkled paper. Without an image such as this, I doubt anyone would believe it could exist.

Salisbury to Exeter Part 4

Jeffery Grayer and Kevin Robertson

(Part 3 appeared in *SW47*.)

Operation

For this, the final article in this series, we now look in detail at the revised signalling arrangements applicable.

In 1966 the route between Salisbury and Exeter consisted of the following signal boxes:

Salisbury West	Crewkerne Gates
Wilton South	Hewish Gates
Dinton	Chard Junction
Chilmark	Broom Gates
Tisbury Quarry Crossing	Axe Gates
Tisbury	Axminster
Tisbury Gates	Seaton Junction
Semley	Honiton Incline
Gillingham	Honiton
Abbey Ford	Sidmouth Junction
Templecombe	Whimple
Millborne Port	Crannaford Gates
Sherbourne	Broad Clyst
Yeovil Junction A	Pinhoe
Yeovil South Junction	Exmouth Junction
Yeovil Junction B	Exeter Central A
Sutton Bingham	Exeter Central B
Crewkerne	

Not all were necessarily manned 24/7, especially the various gate boxes but even so, a considerable manpower resource was represented. The intention of singling the line (also by reducing the number of signal boxes) was to reduce costs in parallel with what would no doubt have been expected to be reduced revenue. We can only be grateful that passengers have been loyal to the route since 1967 and that passenger numbers have increased steadily over the years despite the motive power difficulties that ensued.

Sunshine at Wilton South. Here was the fringe between the Southern and Western Regions, the 'South' designation gibe to separate the station from the WR Wilton station on their line between Salisbury and Westbury.

Steam shuttle between the stations at Yeovil, M7 No 30129 in charge.

It is perhaps too much to hope for a full return to a double track main line and a headboard carrying 'Atlantic Coast Express' but with bi-directional working not available in some parts, we might perhaps one day see some faster trains operating and overtaking slower services by this expedient.

Back at the time of the WR takeover, Salisbury West and Wilton South remained under the control of the Southern Region with the remainder of the signal boxes now under WR control. Prior to singling of the route, the two boxes at Exeter had also been amalgamated with 'B' box closed.

The new signalling for the singling scheme was from a concept devised by Maurice Leech, the CS&TE of the WR, and designed in the Reading S&T drawing office. It was tested by personnel from the same office with a test rig set up in the signal works – at the time still in Caversham Road, Reading – to confirm the new circuitry. Andy MacGregor had the responsibility for developing what became known as WR Tokenless Block, and believed to be some time before the Scottish Region adopted a similar, but not identical system.

The whole route between Wilton South and Pinhoe was now divided into six sections:

Wilton South to Gillingham

Gillingham to Templecombe

Templecombe to Sherborne

Sherborne to Chard Junction

Chard Junction to Honiton

Honiton to Pinhoe

The block system utilised was to a new system designated 'tokenless block', designed to operate over 200lb/mile overhead copper wire using earth returns. No bells were used with telephones, instead being used to pass train codes from one signal box to the next. The block instruments were modified standard WR permissive block type, described by Michael Upton as, "…a typical WR economy measure – even though not much of the original remained after the conversion!" Partly this was done as labour was still comparatively cheap and paid for out of 'overheads' whereas new equipment had to come out of 'projects', hence lots of labour use was encouraged; the other point being there were a lot of these types of instruments redundant as the system contracted.

Wilton South to Gillingham

This was the first section to be converted to single line.

Wilton South signal box was relocked but retained the existing Stevens locking frame. This had the particularly unusual combination of levers lettered/numbered 'A-B-C-1-2-3-4-5-6-7A-7-7B-8-9-10'. *(Believed accurate from the memory of Andy McGregor.)*

The signal box at DInton was closed and replaced by a ground frame providing access to the MoD depot at Chilmark. Teffont Mill Crossing, previously operated from Dinton, was converted to red/ green miniature lights but retained two sets of rails across it; one was the main up/down running line, the other the siding to Chilmark.

This type of crossing with red and green lights had first been introduced by the WR at Crofton between Bedwyn and Savernake.

Chilmark Crossing signal box, together with Tisbury Quarry Crossing box, were both closed and at the latter the crossing was again converted to miniature red/green lights. At Tisbury Gates again the signal was closed and the crossing became automatic half-barrier. Semley signal box was also closed.

A casualty under its old name of Sidmouth Junction but now surviving under the name of Feniton.

Gillingham to Templecombe

Gillingham signal box was retained but the existing Westinghouse 'A3' frame was relocked. A 'King' lever was provided to enable the box to switch out, meaning in a quiet time the 26 miles between Wilton South and Templecombe could be operated as one section.

Abbey Ford signal box was closed whilst an addition was that of an occupation crossing at Ashford which was provided with miniature red/green lights

Templecombe to Sherborne

The signal box at Templecombe was relocked, a Westinghouse 'A2' type frame dating from 1938 installed but reduced with a far smaller number of levers, just 16 instead of the previous 60. (Far fewer levers as with the S&D also closed the connections to this route were redundant. Hence the redundant signal box space became the new station booking office.) The Up line at Templecombe was converted to a single line with the former Down line now bi-directional utilising a modified tokenless block instrument to keep to instruments of the same type.

Milborne Port signal box was closed.

Sherborne to Chard Junction

At Sherborne the Westinghouse 'A2' type frame was relocked.

Further along at Yeovil Junction, 'A' signal box was closed with the connection to Pen Mill now worked by a ground frame. Yeovil South Junction, on the line to Castle Cary, was also closed and the line to Pen Mill singled. Pen Mill signal box, with its original GWR Vertical Tappet 5-bar frame, required some locking alterations.

The signal boxes at Sutton Bingham and Crewkerne were closed. At Crewkerne Gates the signal box was closed with the gates converted to AHB operation monitored from Chard Junction. Special arrangements were made for services in the down direction due to the close proximity of Crewkerne station and the level crossing. The home and distant signals here were worked from Chard Junction with the circuits going over reed equipment.

Another AHB conversion was at Hewish Gates with the former signal box closed.

Chard Junction to Honiton

At Chard Junction the Stevens lever frame was relocked, the line to Chard also recovered. AHBs replaced the signal boxes controlling the crossings at Broom Gates and Axe Gates, both monitored from Chard.

The archetypal view of Seaton Junction from the road bridge which crosses the line. A WR 'Warship' gets away towards Salisbury and Waterloo and passes the wonderful LSWR bracket with its co-acting arms.

At Axminster the signal box was closed and the level crossing here converted to AHB operation monitored from a room in the station building. This also controlled home/distant signals in both directions. The Lyme Regis branch was recovered.

A similar situation occurred at Seaton Junction where the box was closed and the branch to Seaton was recovered. Honiton incline signal box was also recovered.

Honiton to Pinhoe

Honiton signal box required a relock to its Westinghouse 'A3' frame. A 'King' lever was also provided to switch it out of circuit if desired; this meant the section could be Chard Junction to Pinhoe – 27 miles.

Andy McGregor recalls, "This signal box (Honiton) was identical in all respects to that at Gillingham. When the work started, each signal box had a cantilever signal with a two-aspect signal on it. All were erected by the signal gang. When they started at the eastern end, it took them one day to erect and finish, including the wiring of the heads to the box. By the time they got to Honiton, it took only three hours. The only problem at Honiton was when on the platform (of the gantry), it overlooked a wall, on which a young lady was sunbathing in the nude... It took three hours to wire the two signal heads..."

The signal box at Sidmouth Junction was closed. (We have no details of the operation of the level crossing here.) The station was renamed Feniton and the former branch to Sidmouth recovered.

Whimple signal box and that at Crannaford Gates were closed with the later lever crossing converted to AHB monitored from Pinhoe. The signal box at Broad Clyst was also closed.

Finally Pinhoe signal box was relocked.

Teething problems

Due to the overhead wires being uninsulated, problems were occurring in some sections. One section was found to have wires thrown across the lines so all wires associated with the block were replaced with insulated wires. These lasted until the 1980s when a further change was made to cables.

Alterations

After a period of time, it was found that the timetable could not be worked for the simple reason of having too few crossing places. Consequently it was decided to reinstate the section between Sherborne and Yeovil Junction as double track. Sherborne signal box was closed and the gates converted to manned barriers worked by the station staff. The existing signals were retained but now worked automatically.

Diesel shuttle, this time between the stations at Yeovil.

In the final days of a double track main line, No 34087 *145 Squadron* arrives at Templecombe, bound for Exeter on what was a decidedly dismal day.

The former 'Yeovil A' signal box was reopened on 1 October 1967 and renamed 'Yeovil Junction'. The locking frame here was not a standard SR type and so in keeping with WR practice a WR VT 5-bar frame previously installed at Bristol East Depot was used, having been cut down to size as necessary.

Operationally the line to Templecombe was worked as a bi-directional single line. That to Yeovil Pen Mill by electric token.

The single line to Chard started at the end of the station but in the mid-1970s it was found difficult to work so the single line was extended to the west end and a new platform introduced.

In February 1988 Pinhoe was closed with the level crossing worked by CCTV from Exmouth Junction and the tokenless block circuits and monitoring of Crannaford also transferred. The line from Exmouth Junction to Exmouth was also singled but retained a passing loop at Topsham. The mechanical frame was also recovered and the whole area worked from a panel. Hewish Crossing was converted to AHB.

After being returned to the Southern area the section from Tisbury to Wilton South was incorporated into Salisbury Panel with a passing loop provided in the Tisbury area. Tisbury Crossing was renamed Tisbury West Crossing. Finally in 2013 the rest of the route to Exeter was transferred to Basingstoke Signalling Centre.

Other changes post-2013 included Gillingham signal box being reclassified as a Ground Frame and Ashford Crossing reduced to a footpath. Templecombe signal box was closed but the working of the one single line and the one bi-directional line was retained. Sherborne Crossing became CCTV but retaining the existing signal configuration.

At Yeovil the renamed Junction signal box was closed but with token working retained on the connection to Pen Mill whilst the signals at the former are now slotted in operation. (Meaning their operation is affected by a neighbouring control point NOT slotted as per the earlier article on signalling at Esher West.) All four crossings at Crewkerne, Hewish Broom and Axe were retained as AHBs.

Chard Junction signal box was closed, although the existing ground frame was retained. Honiton signal box was also closed.

Finally a two and three-quarter mile section of line through Axminster was doubled but worked as two separate bi-directional lines. The crossing at Axminster was retained but is now worked as CCTV.

Acknowledgements: Andy McGregor and Michael Upton.

PRIVATE AND NOT FOR PUBLICATION

BR.31400/2

Notice No. S.2510

BRITISH RAILWAYS

(WESTERN REGION)

(For the use of employees only)

SALISBURY—EXETER, SINGLING OF LINE

Occupation etc. arrangements in connection with the introduction of Stage 2 (Templecombe to Chard Junction) of the Salisbury—Exeter Singling of Line Scheme.

PRELIMINARY WORK—SATURDAY, 29th APRIL, to SATURDAY, 6th MAY (inclusive)

Saturday, 29th April

All track circuits between Templecombe and Chard Junction inclusive will be given up to the Chief Signal Engineer from 08 00 hours until the commencement of the main occupation. All Distant signals will be maintained at Caution.

Sunday, 30th April

At Yeovil Junction "A"

Occupation of the locking frame will be given to the Chief Signal Engineer at 08 00 hours to permit locking alterations to be carried out.

Main line signals and points will be disconnected and points will be worked by hand until they are spiked out of use or converted to Ground Frame or Hand operation in the main occupation.

At Yeovil Junction "B"

The signal box, together with all associated signals and signalling equipment will be recovered at 08 00 hours.

The connections from Down Local Line to Down Through, also from Up Through to Up Local Line will be spiked, clipped and padlocked set for the Up or Down Local Line.

All other points will be spiked, clipped and padlocked out of use until recovered or converted to hand operation.

At Hewish Gates

The signal box will be reduced in status to a Ground Frame. All signals with the exception of the Up and Down Main Distant and Home Signals, will be recovered. All points will be spiked, clipped and padlocked in the normal position pending recovery. The existing level crossing gates will be retained and will be worked by a Crossing Keeper.

The existing block sections:—
        Yeovil Junction "A"—Yeovil Junction "B"
        Yeovil Junction "B"—Hewish Gates
        Hewish Gates   —Chard Junction
will be superseded by the new block sections:—
        Yeovil Junction "A"—Chard Junction

EMU Pictorial
From the Archives of Graham Smith

We are once again delighted to include some further images from the archive of the late Graham Smith courtesy of Richard Sissons.

As before with Graham's work there is a paucity of information save that which may be gleaned from the actual image. We are grateful to Mike King for assisting in attempting to identify locations but if we have missed one out or made an error, do please let us know so this can be corrected in 'Rebuilt'.

How does the bingo caller call it? Something like '5 and 9 the Brighton line'; somehow no equally rhyming term comes to mind with the headcode '15'! Instead we can state this is 4-LAV No 2940 working a London Bridge to Brighton via Redhill stopping service, possibly recorded near to Haywards Heath.

Similar set, similar working and possibly near to Balcombe tunnel.

2-HAL No 2657 with full yellow end arriving at St Leonards with '18' headcode, possibly an Ore to Brighton service.

Far easier this time, the unmistakeable outline of 4-RES No 3067 leaning to the curve on the approach to Clapham Junction but with the slightly unusual Waterloo to Guildford route number.

A pair of HAP sets, No 5604 leading, recorded at Gillingham, a service from Charing Cross.

Eight car formation north of Patcham tunnel – the A27 now crosses the line at this point. The headcode '12' indicates a Brighton-Victoria via Redhill stopper.

Another 2-HAL, this one No 2630, arriving into London Road station at Brighton from the direction of Lewes/Eastbourne. The signals are for Kemp Town Junction which was just beyond Ditchling Road tunnel.

A light load for an unidentified E50xx electric leaving Herne Bay. The code '07' was for a Cannon Street to Ramsgate via Swanley and Chatham service.

There was something special, it seems to the photographer, about the 4-LAV sets, unit 2926 at Clapham Junction, which will soon depart on the last leg of its journey to Victoria. Definitely an off-peak working. (With apologies for the crease on part of the negative.)

Two-car suburban EPB set No 5734 at Sanderstead. Some indication of the traffic that might be expected at busier times comes from the 9-10 car 'stop' boards.

Also at Herne Bay, 4-BEP No 7006 on a Victoria to Ramsgate via Herne Hill and Chatham train.

Less than ideal conditions for a third-rail electric at Gravesend.

One cf the pair of 'Hornbys', either No 20001 or sister engine 20002, on what is probably a Newhaven boat train.

Finally, busy times at London Bridge. E5015 appears to be on a stock working with a Pullman 'Holiday Coach' and some vans whilst a D65xx (Class 33) shunts stock at the station.

Bishopstone Station:
A Military Strongpoint?

David Larkin

While researching a hypothetical model railway on the South Coast, I came across the rather curious station of Bishopstone, between Newhaven and Seaford. Designed in 1936 and intended to serve a housing estate which was not in fact built until well after World War 2, it was opened in September 1938. Ostensibly following closely the designs of Charles Holden for London Transport, e g Arnos Grove and Bourds Green, the addition of military features in 1940 have resulted in this building being given Grade II Listed status.

Little appears to be known of the reasons behind the 1940 additions but descriptions such as 'gun slits' in a 'pill-box' seem not to tell the whole story. I was born in North Kent and grew up in a village with a number of pill-boxes. These formed a defence line where adjacent pill-boxes could support each other. As far as I know, there are no other such structures anywhere near Bishopstone station.

The location of the station building is not really suitable for a defensive point. As will be seen, the approach on the northern side is uphill and neither slot looks directly down the slope. The station is built on the side of a cutting, beyond which is a significant sloping field before reaching the road and the beach; the slots on this side are mirror images of the northern pair and do not look directly towards the beach.

The road approach to Bishopstone, substantially built in the style of the 1930s, or intended as dual purpose with a more sinister secret?
All images David Larkin

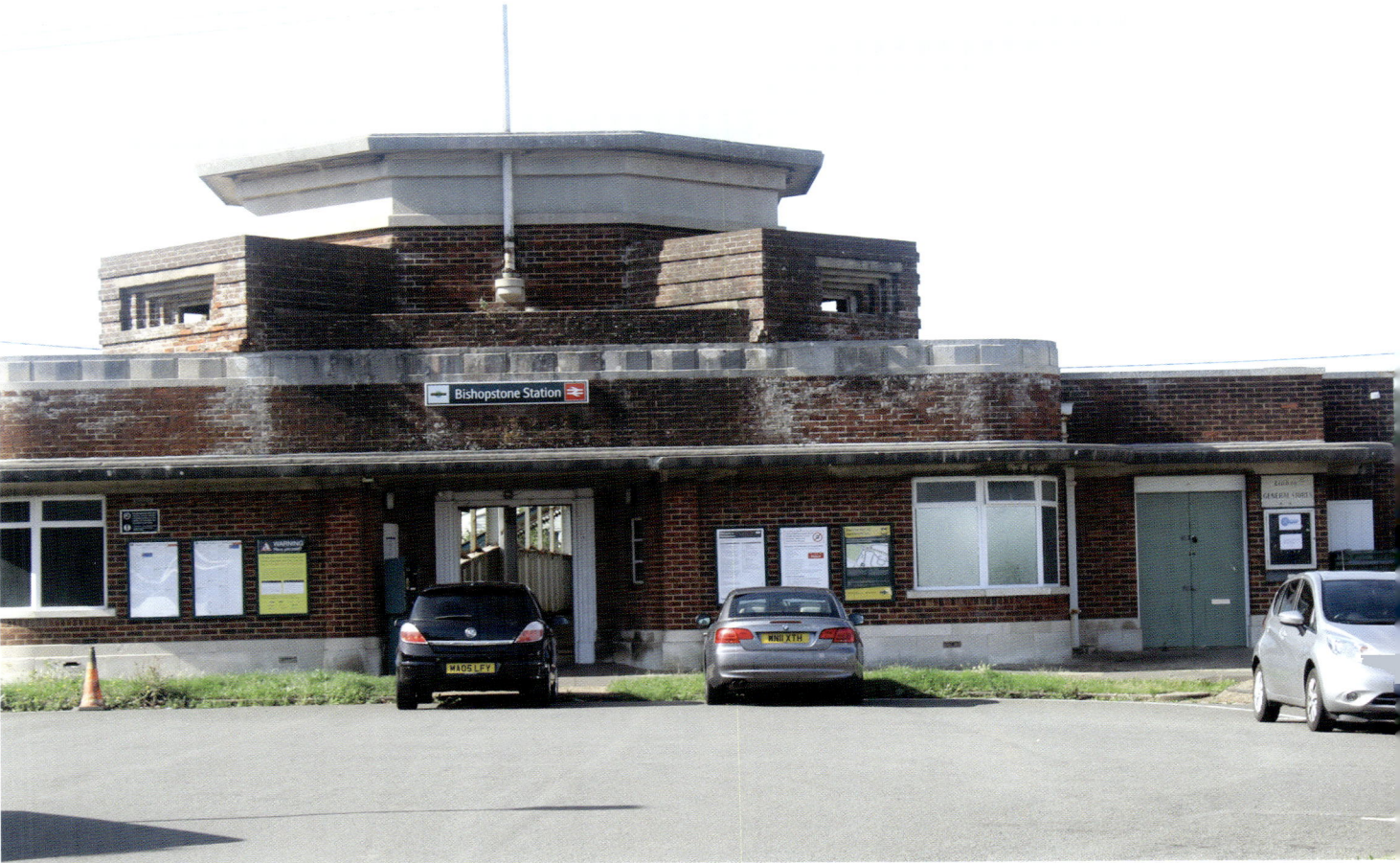

Seen from a closer perspective and the dual purpose becomes ever more unclear.

The north-eastern look out. As will have been gathered from the previous images, there was a similar look-out on the south-east side.

From the station with a commanding view across the breakwater of Newhaven harbour. One might be tempted to consider Captain Mainwaring at this point but it must be said a suitable weapon fired from here could have been a useful (even if perhaps temporary) deterrent.

Towards Newhaven Harbour.

Above: **In the opposite direction, towards Seaford.**

Right: **The slightly unusual encased metal footbridge; perhaps providing more perceived rather than actual protection.**

It is not certain whether the footbridge over the cutting and the stairs down to the platforms were part of the original design but the construction is, to my mind, rather more substantial than warranted for a small, rural station.

Finally, none of the supposed 'gun slits' have clear views downwards and they are not big enough for anything more than a rifle or possibly a Bren gun.

If the views along the branch line itself are considered, the view to the west offers unrivalled views of Newhaven and its harbour. To the east is a deep cutting.

It is therefore my considered opinion that this station was intended to be an artillery observation post to be used in the defence of Newhaven in the event of a German landing with the guns, possibly rail-mounted, being located in the cutting facing west. The station building was to be used as a command building with vision slits, rather than 'gun slits', for all-round observation and the station buildings and footbridge were to afford some protection to the gun crews and their officers.

There would have been other defensive works, such as infantry trenches and anti-aircraft positions, but these would all have been swept away when the housing estate was subsequently built.

Two 19th Century LBSCR Coaches

Ian White

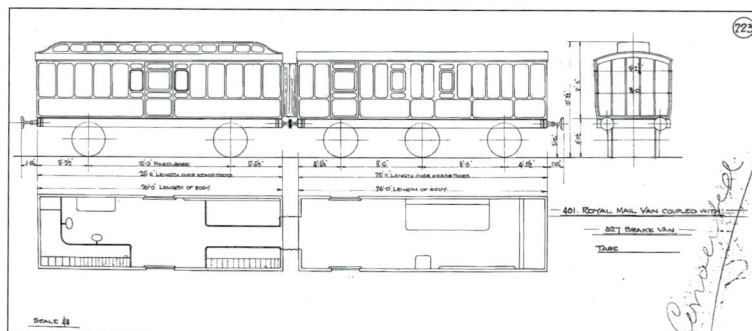

LB&SCR Mail Van: Three of these clerestory mail vans were built in 1878 and they were given numbers in the Second-Class carriage series (Nos 401-403). They ran on 4-wheeled wooden underframes which were to the same dimensions as the standard carriages of the day, that is 26ft long with a 15ft wheelbase. Like other carriages, the body would have been panelled with Honduran mahogany and varnished, but unlike other carriages they carried the "VR" cipher and Royal coat of arms. The wheels were of the wooden type based on the Mansell design, but to a modified pattern patented in 1875 by William Stroudley, the LB&SCR's Locomotive and Carriage Superintendent. Two of the Mail Vans (Nos 402-3) were transferred to service stock and used as Stores Vans. According to the accounts that happened in 1898 but the service register carries pencil notes of 1887 and 1888, and they were marked in one carriage register as "broken up" in 1898. The earliest surviving diagram book was issued at about that same date and it allocated the surviving mail van (No401) to D48. In 1902 No401 was gangway connected to a modified 6-wheeled brake van (No327), described in the brake van registers as a "tender", and this ensemble was allocated to D223 in the final LB&SCR diagram series. As far as is known, no original paper version of the diagram has survived but the diagrams were copied to aperture cards (a format similar to microfilm), and the cards now belong to the Historical Model Railway Society; the D223 diagram is given here (HMRS drawing No2172). Mail van No401 and its tender were transferred to surplus stock in 1920 and appear to have been withdrawn very soon after that.

Above and middle: **LB&SCR Saloon No592:** In 1877 both the LB&SCR and LSWR had built 6-wheeled Royal saloons with domed roofs, and they must have had very spacious interiors when compared to the standard roof heights of the time. The LB&SCR built another 16 First-class saloons in 1882 with the same unusual roof shape, and they displayed the company coat of arms. Four of the saloons were built in Brighton Works but the other 12 were built on contract by Brown Marshalls, who built them to three separate designs specified by the LB&SCR. The original Brown Marshall drawings passed to the Metro-Cammell drawing collection which is now owned by the Historical Model Railway Society, and the drawing applicable to No592 is given here (HMRS drawing No24218). The underframe drawings have not survived, which is a great pity as many of these carriages ran on a Cleminson flexible chassis, a system that allowed the sideways movement of the centre axle to steer the end wheels when going around a curve. According to the LB&SCR diagrams these 30ft long carriages had a wheelbase of 20ft but the SR diagrams noted that those on Cleminson trucks had a wheelbase of 22ft, and this photograph clearly shows the 22ft wheelbase. No592 was one of the Brown Marshall examples and the late 1890s diagram book allocated it to D19, but in 1906 it was re-graded as Second-class saloon No467, and the final diagram series called that D142. It was withdrawn in 1919 but some of the other dome roofed saloons lasted until 1925.

Right: Further photographs and drawings of both the mail vans and saloons can be found in Volume 2 of "LB&SCR Carriages", by Ian White, Simon Turner and Sheina Foulkes, which was published in 2016 by Kestrel Railway Books (ISBN 978-1-905505-36-4). Volume 1 by the same authors was published by Kestrel in 2014 and described the 4- and 6-wheeled standard passenger stock (ISBN 978-1-905505-35-7). Volume 3, written by Ian White and published by the Historical Model Railway Society, described the bogie carriage designs up to 1907 (ISBN 978-1-64516-144-8). The final volume, planned to be published by HMRS in 2021, will describe the remaining bogie passenger stock and the numerous Pullmans operated by the LB&SCR.

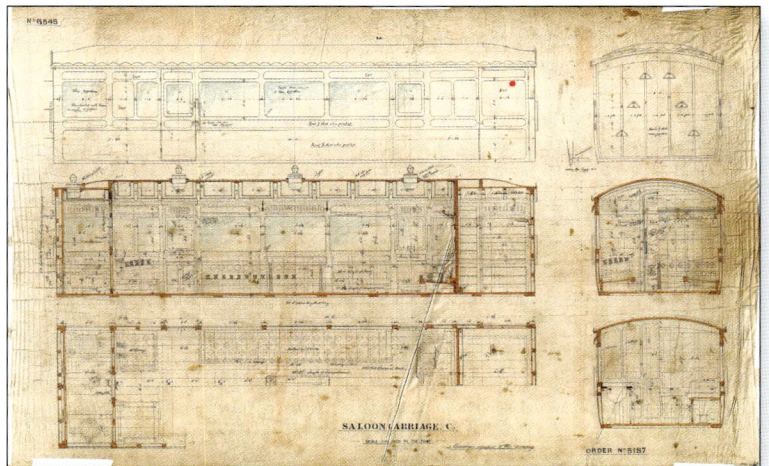

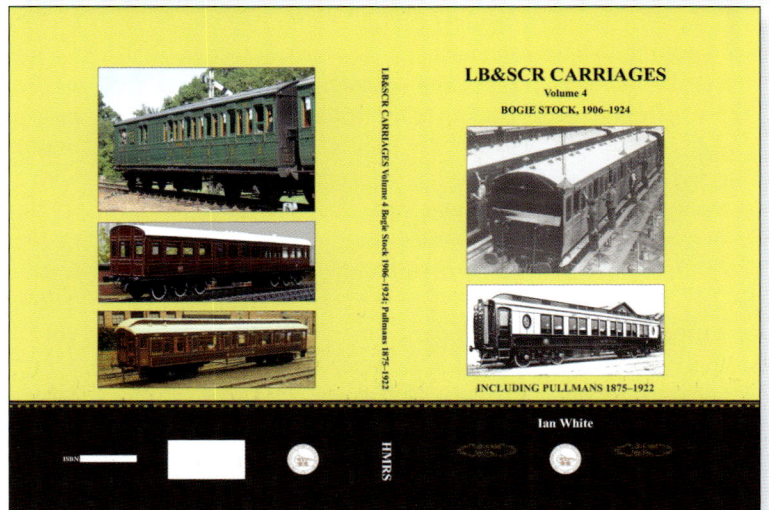

Oil Fuel Firing in the 1920s

Harold Holcroft

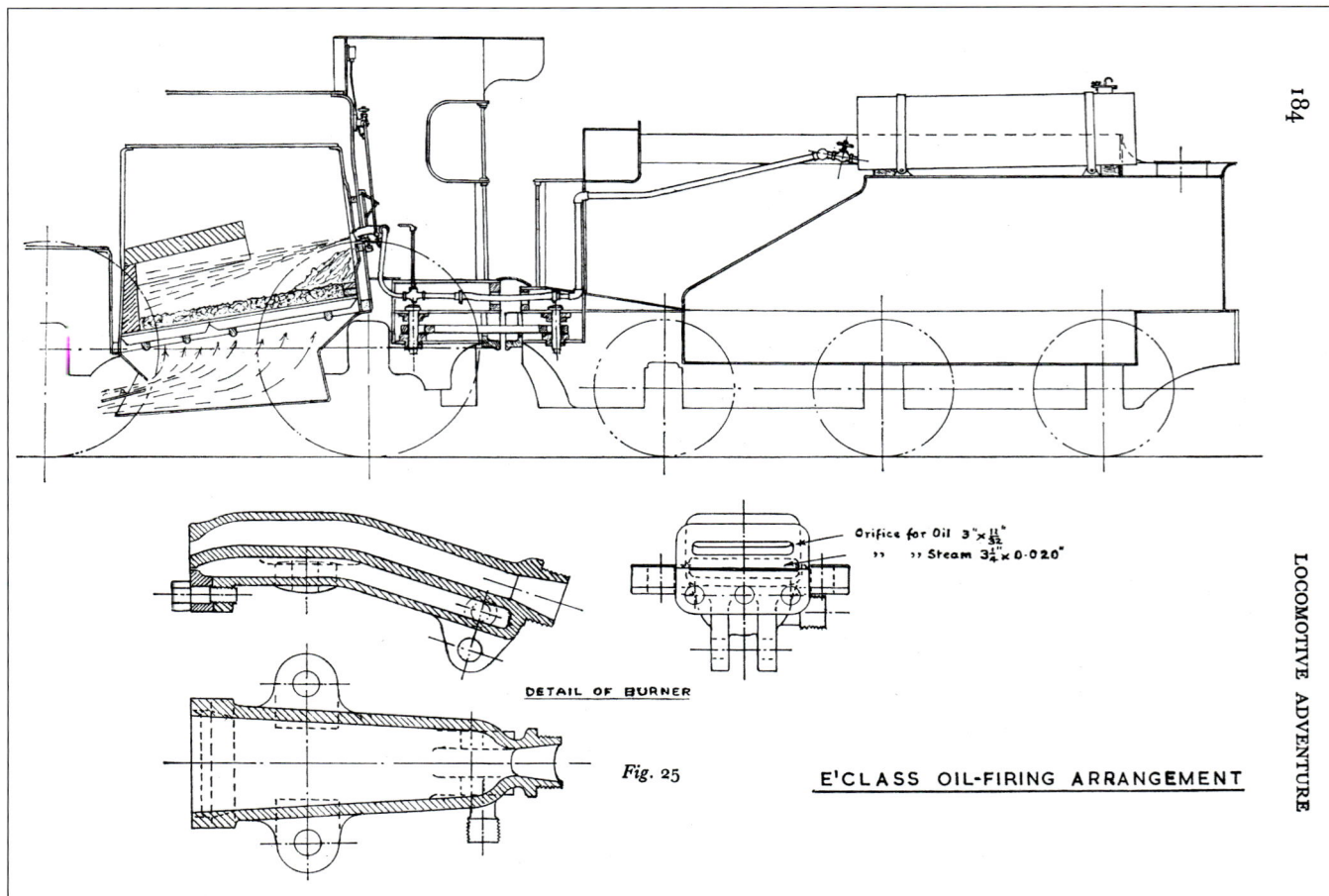

Orifice for Oil 3"×$\frac{11}{32}$"
" " Steam 3$\frac{1}{4}$"×0·020"

DETAIL OF BURNER

Fig. 25

E'CLASS OIL-FIRING ARRANGEMENT

The name Harold Holcroft (1882-1973) will, I am sure, be familiar to many readers of 'SW'. (If for any reason it is not then shame on you!)

Holcroft was a professional engineer who trained at Wolverhampton before coming to the notice of Churchward and moving to Swindon where he had some input into the Churchward 43xx 2-6-0 type before moving to Ashford as assistant to Maunsell and where he was again involved in locomotive design, contributing to Maunsell's own 2-6-0 classes. His Wiki entry https://en.wikipedia.org/wiki/Harold_Holcroft refers to him having collaborated with Gresley on the latter's conjugated valve gear used on the LNER 3-cylinder types, although how working for the LNER and potentially for the Southern at the same time was arrived at is not completely explained.

Returning though to his time on the Southern, Holcroft remained working for Maunsell until the latter retired in 1937; whether he had actually court ambition to the CME's post is not clear but we do know he remained in a senior position under Bulleid until retiring aged 64 in 1946.

Subsequent to that time he was involved with the Institute of Civil Engineers and in 1963 had the first of what would be his two volume autobiography *Locomotive Adventure* published by Ian Allan. This first book was subtitled *Fifty Years with Steam*. His second book, Part 2, *Running Experiences* followed in 1965, all the more credible when it is considered he was by this time already an octogenarian. (Wiki refers to a further unpublished manuscript residing at the NRM entitled 'Life with locos', but that does sound in some ways similar to Vol 2 so may in fact be one and the same. One day we hope to be able to check that out. Both Volume 1 and Volume 2 are heavily orientated towards the Southern and as such are well worth a read, or re-read as the case may be.)

On the Southern it might be fair to refer to a lot of Holcroft's work as being something akin to that of an 'Outdoor Assistant' to the CME. A trusted man tasked with running trials and experimentation. Certainly Volume 2 refers to numerous such events including the subject of what follows, 'Oil fuel Firing'.

We should also make it abundantly clear that the 'Oil fuel Firing' that is the subject of what follows is that which occurred *prior* to the more widely known episode of 1946-1948. Indeed, this earlier period is nowadays almost forgotten although in Volume 2 Holcroft describes 'chapter and verse' the trials and tribulations he experienced. It is therefore long overdue for re-publication.

If we add to this the fact that 'Southern Way Special No 17', scheduled for October 2020 (but recall the Introduction to this issue), is devoted entirely to the 1946-1948 oil burning locomotives and installations, consequently Holcroft's article on earlier times serves as an excellent way to prepare the reader for 'Special 17' and what is to follow later in 2020. Be assured it does not duplicate at all what will appear in 'Special 17', there was simply no room for both to be included!

Indeed, what makes Holcroft's piece all the more interesting is that he is not describing the oil firing as occurred in 1946-48, but what were the earlier runs in the 1920s when a mixture of oil AND coal was combined. In 1946-48 the engines just burnt oil, Holcroft's experiences were based on the earlier method.

This is also likely to be not just a comprehensive record of these workings so far as the Southern (and the SE&CR) was concerned, but probably representative of similar workings that occurred elsewhere around the same time. Indeed, it is probably the only surviving detailed record of the coal/oil mix. (Unless you know different, in which case do please tell us.)

Unfortunately, what is missing are illustrations. Holcroft has none in his book and we have struggled to find any. For that I ask the readers forbearance.

To continue and from now on in Holcroft's words written in 1965; 'The conventional, or "Stephenson", multi-tubular locomotive boiler will not only consume a great variety of solid fuels in its firebox but is adaptable to firing by liquid fuels. In some parts of the world oil is more readily obtainable than coal, especially in the region of the oilfields, and oil-fired locomotives are to be found there. Some countries without suitable supplies of indigenous fuels of their own import oil for locomotive purposes largely because of the ease with which it can be brought in by tanker vessels, discharged, handled and transported on land with the minimum of labour. In Great Britain, with its large reserves of good coal suitable for locomotive purposes, oil firing is uneconomic other than in a few exceptional cases. For instance, the Great Eastern Railway fitted up a few of their express locomotives with apparatus on the Holden system to usefully consume a by-product of their oil gas works for which there was only a limited use, and so save the equivalent in coal. The only other call for the adoption of oil firing in this country has been during prolonged coal strikes leading to stoppage of normal coal supplies. In case of necessity—the essential traffic could be kept moving and communications maintained without coal by means of oil firing after all coal stacks had been exhausted; in this sense it was a precautionary measure to be explored in advance. When this situation threatened, various railways in the country took tentative steps. On the SE&CR one engine each of three classes was fitted up as a prototype, to find by trial the best layout and to gain experience in service, making any modifications to get the optimum results and the maximum of reliability. Once this was arrived at it would have been possible to have mass-produced all parts and piping from detailed drawings and so rapidly convert a number of locomotives. The system adopted by the SE&CR in 1921 was that developed by the Midland Railway at Derby, as it was the simplest and needed the minimum of alteration for the conversion and the least amount of brickwork. The normal ashpan, dampers and firebars were retained. A flash wall of firebrick was built against the firebox tube plate between the underside of the brick arch and the firebars. Two layers of firebricks, 5in. high by 3in. wide, were laid on the firebars against the other firebox plates, leaving a large rectangular space which was filled in by broken firebricks and limestone above the firebars and level with the brick edging. The burner, which was of the weir type, was fixed on the bottom of the firehole and was inclined at an angle towards the flash wall. The burner had two narrow slits about 3in. wide, the lower one being a steam jet. The oil flowing from the upper slit in the form of a ribbon dropped on the steam and was pulverised so that it ignited in a flame. The firehole was closed by sliding doors cut away to fit around the burner to which steam and oil were piped through control valves and fitted with a steam pressure gauge. The supply of oil was carried in two long cylindrical reservoirs, one at each side of the tender longitudinally. There were filling holes and stop valves controlling the pipe between engine and tender, with flexible connection. In the case of tank engines the single reservoir was mounted on top of the bunker transversely. The oil used was gas oil or equivalent of low viscosity at normal ranges of atmospheric temperatures. Although costing more than crudes of high viscosity, it was more reliable and obviated the necessity for heaters on the supply line to reduce viscosity to a suitable degree before reaching the burner. Besides the oil flame, a little coal was burnt in the back corners of the grate. It covered two triangular areas through which excess air could otherwise find its way unhindered through the firebar covering. The coal fire not only checked this but made use of it for combustion. The presence of this small fire enabled the flame to be re-lit after a short stoppage, and it helped to maintain firebox temperature when the oil flame was shut down for longer periods and so helped to reduce or obviate leakages at tubes and stays. The coal used did not have to be of good quality; loose coal from the depleted stacks or even refuse coal picked up would suffice.

The first engine to be fitted up at Ashford in May 1921 was No 329, an H class Wainwright 0-4-4 type tank. No 503 had been selected in the first place but repairs to it were not finished in time. No 329 was tried out on light engine running between Ashford and Maidstone East and back. My first run with it in service was on the 8.36am stopping train from Ashford to Maidstone on 15 June; the weather was fine and hot and the load 103 tons tare.

Coal fire on grate at Ashford: 100lb. approx.
Coal fire on grate at Maidstone: 50lb. approx.
Added on journey: 100lb. approx.
Total coal burnt: 150lb. approx.
Time 47 min. Distance 19 miles. Coal consumed per minute = 3.2lb.: per mile 7.9lb.
Coal added during stop at Maidstone: 240lb. approx.
Coal in firebox at start back: 100lb. approx.
Coal consumed to maintain steam while standing: 140lb. approx.
Time standing 1 hr. 20 min. Coal consumed per minute of standing time: 1.7lb.
Return was at 10.43am with a load of 87 tons.
Coal fire on grate at Maidstone: 100lb. approx.
Coal added on journey: 50lb. approx.
Fire on grate at Ashford: Nil.
Coal used on journey: 150lb.
Time 40 min. Distance 19 miles. Coal used: = 3.7lb. per minute or 7 9lb. per mile.
Oil used on up journey: 55gal.
Oil used on down journey: 47gal.
Weight of oil used @ 81½lb./gal. 865lb. approx.
Weight of oil used per mile: 22.7lb. approx.
Weight of oil used per minute: 10lb. approx.
Ratio of oil to coal in running: 865 divided by 300 = 2.88:1.
Rate of oil to coal on calorific basis of 18.5—BTU for oil and 13,000 BTU for coal is 2.88 x 18,500 divide by 13,000 = 4.1:1.

Therefore, approximately, the oil accounted for 80 percent of heat units required for steaming. Steam pressure and water level in the boiler were well maintained. The steam pressure for burner ranged from 30 to 35lb. per sq.in., and the oil control cock at burner was rather less than half open. It was regulated slightly one way or the other to keep the smoke from the chimney to a light grey in colour. (Unless a little smoke was visible it would not be possible to know if air was in excess.) This test was very satisfactory. My next run on No 329 was on 28 June with the 7.7am stopping train Ashford to Maidstone. Weather fine, hot and dry: load 88 tons tare. Coal used was rather more while running but the same as before during standing at Maidstone, but the oil used was only 35½gal.

The return was with the 8.45am ex-Maidstone and the oil used 39gal. and more coal was used than before. This trip was less satisfactory as oil was economised at the expense of coal, the oil control cock not being opened so much. The run was repeated with the same train on 30 June. The burner had been changed; instead of a wide slot for the oil the passage was ribbed longitudinally so that the oil issued in a number of streams instead of as a ribbon. This not only economised in oil, but less coal was needed to keep up full pressure and water level. It was a better result all round.

The next to be fitted up was No 165, E1 class 4-4-0. After trial running my first trip with this engine was on 21 June with the 7.47am ex-Ashford to Cannon Street, stopping all stations to Tonbridge, then Hildenborough, Sevenoaks and London Bridge. The weather was drizzly with greasy rails causing much slipping. Load from Ashford to Tonbridge was 171 tons tare. Here the load

was increased to 241 tons. The average speed Knockholt to Southwark Park was 65mph. Return was with the 11am Charing Cross to Ashford via Maidstone East, stopping at London Bridge, Hither Green and Maidstone. Steaming was very good, but the oil valve could not be opened more than ½ without causing smoke, so that coal consumption was high to make up for the deficiency. This working was repeated on 29 June; weather being fine, hot and dry. Load to Tonbridge 168 tons and 244 tons to Cannon Street. From Charing Cross to Ashford it was 234 tons. Steaming was good, but again too much coal was needed. On the up journey fuel consumed was 18.0lb. oil and 13.7lb. of coal per mile. For the return 17.4lb. of oil and 15.2lb. of coal per mile, the ratios being 1.32:1 and 1.15: 1 respectively. The long sloping grate did not lend itself to the change as did the deeper and 'squarer' firebox of the H class engine. We had some discussion on this result and decided to try some modification to No 165, to reduce excess air in the back corners and so need to burn less coal. Accordingly, on 7 July No 165 took the 8.35am stopping train from Ashford to Ramsgate Town with 114 tons, weather being showery. Return was with the 10.29am ex-Ramsgate with 173 tons, stopping all stations. The result was a consumption of 16.7lb. of oil and 14.1lb. of coal for the outward journey and 21.6lb. and 8.7lb. respectively for the return. Overall, the ratio was improved so the engine was put on the same working as on 21 June, loads being 194 tons ex-Ashford, made up to 302 tons at Tonbridge. Return was with 266 tons ex-Charing Cross. On this occasion coal was weighed, 40cwt. being put on the tender and 15cwt. taken off after arrival back at Ashford, consumption being 25cwt.; of this 560lb. was used in lighting up and raising steam and 200lb. used while standing in London, leaving 2,040lb. consumed while running. On the up journey fuel consumed was 21.0lb. of oil and 17.8lb. of coal per mile on the outward trip, 15.3lb. of oil and 18.1lb. of coal per mile on return. The previous day's more promising result was not repeated with the heavier loading, so further modifications were contemplated, such as bricking over some part of the grate at the back corners. Unlike in the case of Nos 329 and 165, Engine No 772, L class 4-4-0, was fitted with the 'Scarab' system of oil burning, which made a complete conversion of the firing and was not a temporary expedient as with the Derby system; it was a straight oil job. In this case the ashpan and bars were removed and a shallow pan put in their place which carried the oil burner and dampers at the front end. The floor had a firebrick lining with air passages below, and holes in the floor distributed the incoming air supply. The flash wall of firebrick was below the level of the firehole and lay against the back plate; the sides were lined to the same height and the front below the normal brick arch, so making a chamber lined with bricks all round and on its floor. There was a small arch below the firehole to protect the door from flame; this was not opened in service but there was a small inspection hole in it for observation to be made. The burner, therefore, was directed from below the foundation ring of the firebox, inclining a little upwards and arrived at the centre of the flash wall. As the burner was steam-operated it could not be started up with the boiler out of steam, so a temporary supply was arranged by standing an engine in steam on an adjacent road. This supply was provided

Concurrent with the oil burning that was taking place on the SECR, the LSWR fitted two N15 4-6-0s to burn oil in 1921 but using the Scarab system. This just involved oil with no subsidiary coal fire involved. Bradley briefly refers to the two engines, Nos 737 and 739 converted in April and June 1921 respectively. They were stationed at Nine Elms for passenger work during the day and heavy goods working at night. Their use, and it might even say their success, was both limited and short lived for No 739 'burst into flames' outside Salisbury shed on 28 July 1921 and did not work again as an oil burner. Both reverted to coal, in September and August 1921 respectively. No 737 is seen here outside Eastleigh Works. We are not told where and how bunkering was achieved.

by breaking the joint at one of the injector supply valves and carrying a pipe across to the connection on the steam supply to the burner. Ignition was by such means as a flame from burning oily cotton waste on the end of a rod. As soon as boiler pressure was raised to about 30lb. per sq.in. the temporary supply could be dispensed with and No 772 could continue with its own supply. After some light engine runs No 772 was put on Ashford—Charing Cross services, as the London to Dover road via Tonbridge and Sevenoaks was the only one the L class could use ex-Ashford due to weight restrictions. My first run on it was on 5 July on the 10.33am train of 255 tons tare to Charing Cross, stopping at Paddock Wood, Tonbridge, Sevenoaks, Orpington, Grove Park, London Bridge and Waterloo. The burner was lit at the shed at 7.15am and by 9.15 pressure stood at 70lb., and by 10.15 it was at full pressure and ready to depart for its train.

Considering the lack of experience in working, the system pressure and water level were satisfactorily maintained on the journey. After arrival at Charing Cross the engine picked up six vans for the Ewer St. Depot where the engine stood for a time with the burner shut off. On opening the firedoor the small brick arch below it was seen to have collapsed on the journey. It was also noted that leakages from tube ends and stay heads were much heavier than with the other two engines when standing, due to larger temperature drop. The matter was reported to Cannon Street running shed and No 772 was called on to go there and await the time when a path could be arranged for its return to Ashford light for repairs to the brickwork.

My next run with the engine was on 11 July with the 10.25am ex-Ashford to Charing Cross with a train of 202 tons, stopping at Paddock Wood, Tonbridge, London Bridge and Waterloo. The weather was hot and dry and steaming was very good, full pressure of 160lb. being sustained over long periods. Oil consumed between Ashford and Charing Cross was 150gal. representing an average of 21.5lb. per mile. The engine proceeded to the Ewer St. Depot for turning and preparation for return. The burner was shut off at 12.45pm and relit at 2.30pm, 79gal. of oil being used in the London Area. No 772 then departed to Charing Cross to work the 3.0pm to Ashford of 221 tons tare, stopping at London Bridge, Sevenoaks and Tonbridge. Steaming was good once more and could have been better with a little practice. Oil used was 153gal. or 22.0lb. per mile. The main supply of air was drawn through by the smokebox vacuum; a little more was induced at the burner. There was no automatic regulation of fuel burning as with a coal fire, so the air supply was adjusted by opening of damper and adjustment of the oil control valve. The latter had 48 graduations between shut and full. It was varied according to demand for steam and its setting was mainly between 17/48 and 14/48; the damper was about ¾ open, but varying plus or minus to suit conditions. Apart from working the injector, the fireman could devote himself to adjustment of oil and air in accordance with pressure and water level fluctuations, and avoiding any emission of smoke in doing so. With a little practice it would have been possible to get almost perfect steaming conditions, for there was no deterioration in the situation as with a coal fire in the accumulating ash and clinker

on the grate. With oil the only likely cause to offset steaming would be a deposit of soot on the tube surfaces due to a smoky flame being allowed to develop. The fitting of a soot blower in the firebox back as an additional mounting would have overcome this by its use during running.

The dispute in the Coal Industry was settled shortly after this so any further experiments in oil firing were called off and train services returned to normal as coal supplies began to arrive. The apparatus on the three engines was taken off and stored in case of another dispute arising in the future. 'Know-how' and experience had been gained and expansion could be more rapid on a second occasion.

The occasion arose five years later when another National Coal Strike was called. During the interval Grouping of the railways had taken place and the CME's Headquarters had been moved to London in the Waterloo offices. As the dispute seemed likely to be prolonged the Trades Union Congress declared a General Strike all over the country on 4 May 1926, with a view to precipitating matters. This collapsed in a short time due to the action of 'John Citizen' who rushed to the aid of the State in keeping essential services going. The miners doggedly carried on alone and a fuel shortage, due to the need to cut down on the rate at which stock piles were diminishing, began to be felt.

Once more some oil firing was to be resumed and as far as the Eastern Section was concerned the former SE&CR at Ashford had all the experience needed to make a fresh start. It was the Western Section which required our attention most. Maunsell sent me post-haste to Derby on 20 May 1926, with a letter addressed to Sir Henry Fowler which I was to hand to him personally. After reading it he sent for Herbert Chambers and instructed him to give me every assistance in getting together the necessary components for despatch to Eastleigh. Needless to say I received every attention and was hospitably entertained. As there was some time before the train for my return to London, D W Sanford was deputed to take me round the shops. All three mentioned often called in at the Waterloo office, so it was a pleasant and friendly affair. Clayton had been sent to Ashford by the Chief to get things moving there. On his return he was very nettled to find that I had been to Derby which he seemed to regard as his special preserve.

However, he got over it during the day and then we set to and discussed the possibility of applying oil firing to the K class 2-6-4 tanks. On 8 June I had a run on No 329, which had been re-equipped, from Ashford to Hastings and back.

After the Grouping became effective in the CME Dept. in the summer of 1923, my activities were for a time largely devoted to matters relating to the fusion of practices between the three Sections, involving much investigation at the various Works and all over the system, and I saw less of the footplate. Also, a Locomotive Testing and Experimental Department was set up to undertake the more routine jobs; nevertheless in 1925, after the move to Waterloo, I was called on by the CME to undertake special missions which involved more running on the footplate. It was in this way that I was sent down to Eastleigh to give them a start on oil firing on the Derby system.

From previous experience the cost of fitting per engine was estimated at £110 and if all materials were to hand the job should not occupy more than 48 hours; dismantling could be done in 8 hours. My instructions were to see that the flexible hose for conveying the oil from tender to engine could not chafe or kink, and an armoured hose 3ft. 10in. long by 1½in. bore was selected from Stores. Care was to be taken that there was a small gap under the flash wall so that the firebars could be removed if necessary. The burner was to be set low and adjusted on each engine independently. In service the engine had to steam well with the second valve of regulator open and the injector on. Also, I had to arrange with the Locomotive Running Department for their footplate inspectors and as many crews as could be conveniently accommodated to go on each trial trip to initiate them into procedure. After that I was to travel with the engines in service to give any further instruction to the crews. On the 10th I was at Eastleigh and had a light run on No E470, D15 class 4-4-0, which was the first to be fitted up there. We went as far as Basingstoke and there collected all the old firebricks

they had for use on further engines to have firebeds of broken brick. I noted that on spotting a distant signal at caution the driver shut off steam at once and applied the brake until speed was considerably reduced well before approaching the stop signal. He said that the engine brake power was on the low side and a light engine might otherwise overrun the signal unless it had a passenger train behind it to pull it up! The LSWR engines of Adams had a powerful steam brake but when Drummond succeeded him he went over to the vacuum brake; it would seem, then, that engine brake block wear was reduced and periods of adjustment lengthened at the expense of Panter's carriage stock. The next day No E470 was put on the midday van train which ran from Eastleigh to Clapham Junction via Virginia Water and Staines, stopping at Basingstoke, Woking and any other point where vans were to be put off or picked up. This train was composed of vacuum-fitted stock running with passenger trains, such as horseboxes, carriage trucks, milk vans, empty passenger stock and saloons working back.

The particulars of the trip are as follows:

		Pressure lb per sq in	Water level in inches	Injector	Remarks
1.37pm	Eastleigh dep.	180	6	Off	
1.51¾	Shawford pass	170	6	On	
		160			6 shovels of coal added
1.58¾	Winchester pass	165	5	On	
		155			6 shovels of coal added
2.16	Micheldever pass	155	5	Off	
2.32	Basingstoke arr.				Vehicle detached here: load reduced to 211 tons
3.11½	Basingstoke dep.	170	6	Off	
3.20½	Hook pass	155	5	On	
3.23½	Winchfield pass	155	4½	Off	
3.28½	Fleet pass	145	4	On	
3.32¼	Farnborough arr.	145	5½	On	Van picked up here
3.39	Farnborough dep.	180	6	Off	
3.47	Brookwood pass	150	4½	On	
3.52¾	Woking arr.	160	6	On	Load reduced to 103 tons
4.18¼	Woking dep.	180	6	Off	
4.23½	Byfleet pass	175	5½	On	
4.28½	Sunbury pass	170	5½	Off	
4.30½	Chertsey pass	160	5½	On	
4.34¼	Virginia Water pass	165	5½	Off	
4.38¼	Egham pass	155	5	On	
4.42	Staines arr.	170	5	Off	Van detached here
4.50½	Staines dep.	165	6	Off	
4.52¾	Ashford pass	175	6	On	
4.56¼	Feltham pass	155	5½	Off	Signal checks
5.03	Twickenham pass	160	6	On	
5.04¼	St Margaret's pass	165	6	Off	
5.07	Richmond arr.	175	5	On	Horse box detached
5.11	Richmond dep.	170	6	Off	
5.15	Mortlake pass	160	6	On	
5.18½	Barnes Junc. pass	150	6	Off	
5.20½	Putney pass	155	6	Off	
5.22¼	Wandsworth Town pass	160	5½	On	
5.24	Clapham Junc. arr.	150	5	On	

Oil consumption

	Miles	Load in tons	Oil used in gallons	Oil use in lb. per Mile
Eastle gh-Basingstoke	25.7	298	104.0	34.3
Basingstoke-Farnborough	14.6	211	41.7	24.3
Farnborough-Woking	8.9	222	20.8	19.9
Woking-Staines	9.8	103	20.8	18.0
Staines-Clapham Junction	15.1	113	20.6	11.7

No E470 was in charge of Driver Cocker, of Nine Elms, and the weight of train behind it for the 18 miles of 1 in 252 up out of Eastleigh to the Litchfield summit and onwards as far as Basingstoke amounted to 298 tons. The oil tank on the tender was of oblong shape, 6ft. 8in. wide, 2ft. 6in. deep and 12ft. 0in. long. It contained 1,250 gallons of oil or 41.6gal. per inch of depth. This was much more convenient for measuring than the two cylindrical tanks used on the Eastern Section and whose capacity per inch of depth varied; also, both tanks had to be gauged by dipstick in case the tender was not standing level. This gave a total consumption of 208.2gal. over 74.1 miles, an average of 23.8lb. per mile for an average load of 208 tons. The heaviest working was from Eastleigh over the first 18 miles for which a full regulator was used with a 25 percent cut-off. The cut-off remained at 25 percent but only the small valve of the regulator was needed for the easier downhill running. Pressure and water level were well maintained and no troubles were experienced. It was a good 'maiden voyage'. Beyond the 12 shovelfuls of coal used between Eastleigh and the summit I could not find in my notes that any coal was used while running, though some may have been added at stops. In any case, No E470 was able to use a large proportion of oil.

On 14 June I caught No E739, N15 class 4-6-0, at Basingstoke, where it had brought up the van train from Eastleigh. It departed at 3.2½.pm with a load of 333 tons and only stopped at Winchfield to pick up a cattle truck; it ran to Clapham Junction via Virginia Water, arriving at 5.50pm. Everything went well, though with this normally heavy loading the timing was very easy. Next day I was with No 415, L12 class 4-4-0, which took the 4.10pm train from Eastleigh to Waterloo via Alton and Aldershot stopping at all stations to Woking, and then fast to Waterloo, Surbiton being the only stop. This was of particular interest to me, being my first time 'over the Alps' as the enginemen called the route diverging from Winchester and re-joining the main line at Pirbright Junction, owing to its hilly nature. The load was 5 bogies weighing 130 tons at the start but 4 more coaches were added at Alton, making 234 tons. On 17 June I picked up No E420, L12 class, at Basingstoke in charge of Driver Francis, of Eastleigh. The load from there consisted of 9 coaches and 14 four-wheeled vehicles, making a total of 423 tons. The job was not as big as it would seem, as it was gentle downhill running, two hours being taken between Basingstoke and Clapham Junction Two horse boxes were put off at Fleet and 4 bogie coaches added at Farnborough. Instead of the usual route via

Virginia Water the run was made wholly on the main line. The reason for this diversion and the number of coaches on the train was probably due to the Aldershot Military Tattoo which was on at the time. Immediately on arriving at Clapham Junction the engine was commandeered to work a special train of empty stock to Waterloo for Aldershot. As the oil burning on the L12 class had not been so successful some alteration was made to No E415 at Nine Elms, and on 19 June I went inside the firebox to get particulars. An extra course of bricks had been added to the top of the arch at the back (high) end which had the effect of making the oil flame take a longer path round the arch and bringing it closer to the backplate and crown. This engine was put on the 9.50am Waterloo— Portsmouth train on 21 June in charge of Driver Watts, of Nine Elms. There were 11 coaches of 290 tons tare.

The run with the 9.50am Waterloo to Portsmouth was repeated on the 25th with 284 tons. The train was very crowded with passengers; there was a struggle for steam at first, due to lack of preparation, but steaming was good from Guildford onwards. The tubes were sanded after passing Clapham Junction; this was done by taking a level shovelful of dry sand and holding it just inside the firehole so that it was swept off by the blast and carried through the tubes, so dispersing any soot on them. On this run a steam pressure of 25lb. to the burner was tried instead of 50lb. as before. There was a signal check after passing Wimbledon. This trial gave oil consumed as about 14.8lb. per mile, and coal used as about 20.6lb. per mile. Not so much oil could be burnt with 25lb. steam pressure, and much more coal than on the previous trip was needed. Return to Waterloo was with 144 tons on stopping train as before.

The L12 class had a very deep firebox and this did not suit oil firing as well as on other classes. I proposed that the grate should be lifted about 9in. above the foundation ring; this was agreed to but could not be put into effect at once as it needed special brackets and comb bars. It was not until 16 September that I went on a trial run with it from Eastleigh to Basingstoke, but it was the last of my oil firing as the 'Lord Nelson' was out of shops and I had to go riding on it. In any case the emergency was over with the coal dispute settled.

Waterloo – Portsmouth 21 June

am		Pressure lb per sq in	Water level in inches	Injector	Coal in shovels
9.50¼	Waterloo dep.	180	6	Off	
9.54	Vauxhall pass	180	5½	On	
9.56	Queens Road pass	180	5½	On	
9.57½	Clapham Junc pass	175	5	On	
9.59	Earlsfield pass	170	4½	On	
10.01½	Wimbledon pass	160	5	On	5
10.09¼	Esher pass	155	3	On	
10.12	Walton pass	140	3	Off	8
10.17	Byfleet pass	145	2½	On	
10.20	Woking pass	150	2	Off	10
10.29	Guildford arr.	150	5	On	6
10.33	Guildford dep.	175	6	Off	6
10.39¾	Farncombe pass	180	6	On	
10.41	Godalming pass	180	6	On	
10.44	Milford pass	175	6	On	7
10.48½	Witley pass	175	6	On	14
10.58½	Haslemere pass	170	4	On	6
11.03½	Liphook pass	150	3	On	
11.12¾	Petersfield arr.	170	5½	Off	13
11.15	Petersfield dep.				
11.29	Rowlands Castle pass	145	4½	On	6
11.33¼	Havant pass	160	5	Off	9
11.42¼	Fratton arr.	170	4½	On	
11.44	Fratton dep.	165	6	Off	
11.47	Portsmouth arr.	160	On	On	
11.51	Portsmouth dep.	175	6	Off	
11.54¼	Portsmouth H. arr.	140	5	On	

Return to Waterloo was with 6 bogies, 132 tons, stopping all stations to Surbiton.

Waterloo – Portsmouth 25 June

am		Pressure lb per sq in	Water level in inches	Injector	Coal in shovels
9.49¼	Waterloo dep.	170	6	Off	6
9.53	Vauxhall pass	150	5½	On	6
9.55	Queens Road pass	145	5	Off	6
9.57¾	Clapham Junc. pass	150	3½	On	
9.59	Earlsfield pass	140	3	On	
10.01¼	Wimbledon pass	140	3	Off	6
10.04	Raynes Park pass	160	3	On	4
10.05¼	Maldon pass	160	2½	On	4
10.08½	Surbiton pass	150	2½	On	27
10.11	Esher pass	150	2	On	11
10.14¼	Walton pass	150	1½	On	7
10.15½	Weybridge pass	160	1½	On	14
10.19¼	Byfleet pass	160	1½	On	6
10.22½	Woking pass	170	3	On	7
10.31	Guildford arr.	175	6	On	7
10.34	Guildford dep.	180	6	Off	5
10.40½	Farncombe pass	180	5½	On	6
10.41¾	Godalming pass	180	5½	On	7
10.45	Milford pass	170	5	On	7
10.48	Witley pass	175	5	On	15
20.58¾	Haslemere pass	170	4½	On	7
11.04¼	Liphook pass	170	5	Off	
11.09¼	Liss pass	165	5	On	7
11.13	Petersfield arr.	170	5	On	
11 15¼	Petersfield dep.	170	6	Off	10
11 20¾	Buriton pass	170	5½	On	
11.29	Rowlands Castle pass	155	5½	On	5
11.32¾	Havant pass	170	5½	Off	
11.41	Fratton arr.	180	5½	On	7
11.43½	Fratton dep.	180	6	Off	
11.46¼	Portsmouth arr.	170	5	On	6
11.51	Portsmouth dep.	180	6	Off	
11.54½	Portsmouth H. arr.	170	5	On	

The Eastern Section had been adding to their oil-fired engines, for I have a note that No A19, E1 class, worked the 9.05am Victoria—Ramsgate train on 23 June, but I did not ride on it as I was travelling down with others to go into the plans for the new Ramsgate station on the site.

The highlight of these oil-burning runs came on 9 July, when No E739, N15 class, worked the *Atlantic Coast Express* between Waterloo and Salisbury and back. Owing to cuts in train services at the time, intermediate stops were introduced at Surbiton, Woking, Basingstoke and Andover in each direction. Tare load of 13 bogies was 350 tons. The up train was an hour late into Salisbury. It consisted of coaches of 311 tons tare.

For the outward and return journeys together the consumption per mile was approximately 18lb. of oil and 11lb. of coal. On a calorific basis this indicates that 70 percent of the steam generated was by oil, as against 80 percent for the H class tank. It was a very satisfactory result and no doubt could have been bettered with a little more experience. The D15 was able to burn a larger percentage of oil than any.

Waterloo – Salisbury 9 July 1926

am		Pressure in lb per sq in	Water level in inches	Injector	Coal in shovels	Steam pressure for Burner in lb per sq ft
11.00	Waterloo dep.	180 B.O.	6	Off		35
11.03½	Vauxhall pass	185	5½	On	8	40
11.08½	Clapham Junc. pass	170	5½	On	5	40
11.10	Earlsfield pass	175	5	Off	4	40
11.12¼	Wimbledon pass	170	5	On		45
11.14	Raynes Park pass	165	5	On	4	45
11.15¼	Maldon pass	175	5	Off		48
11.18½	Surbiton arr.	180 B.O.	5	On	1	20
11.19½	Surbiton dep.	185	6	Off		40
11.24½	Esher pass	160	5½	On	4	35
11.27	Walton pass	170	4	Off	6	45
11.30½	Weybridge pass	165	3½	On	4	42
11.33¼	Byfleet pass	165	3	On		41
11.37	Woking arr.	150	2½	On	8	39
?	Woking dep.	160	5½	Off		43
11.44	?	170	4½	On	15	39
11.47	Brookwood pass	165	4½	On	9	40
11.54¾	Farnborough pass	185 B.O.		Off		
11.59	?	160	5½	Off		41
12.00½ pm Fleet pass		170	5	Off	4	45
12.05	Winchfield pass	155	4½	Off	6	40
12.08¼	Hook pass	165	3	On	5	47
12.15½	Basingstoke arr.	170	3	On		32
12.17¾	Basingstoke dep.	180	6	Off	9	40
12.23½	Worting Junc. pass	170	4½	On	3	41
12.26½	Oakley pass	165	3½	On	3	40
12.30¾	Overton pass	160	3	On	4	40
12.34¾	Whitchurch pass	150	2½	Off	4	40
12.36½	Hurstbourne pass	150	3	On	6	43
12.42¾	Andover arr.	175	3½	On	5	35
12.44	Andover dep.	180	3½	Off	8	38
12.55	Grateley pass	170	4½	On	6	43
1.01¾	Porton pass	160	2½	On	4	40
1.05	Tunnel Junc. pass	150	3	On		32
1.08	Salisbury arr.	145		On		

Estimated oil used 187gal. or 19.0lb. per mile. Estimated coal used 1,128lb. or 13.5lb. per mile.

Salisbury – Waterloo 8 July

am		Pressure in lb per sq in	Water level in inches	Injector	Coal in shovels	Steam pressure for Burner in lb per sq ft
3.20	Salisbury dep.	175	6	Off	16	35
3.38¼	Porton pass	180	5½	On	9	42
?	P.Way Check.	155	5	Off		
3.47	Grateley pass	170	4	On		42
3.54¾	Andover arr.	170	5	On	4	34
3.58	Andover dep.	185 B.O.	6	Off	6	38
4.06½	Hurstbourne pass	160	5½	On		40
4.09	Whitchurch pass	175	5	On		42
4.16	Overton pass	150	5	Off		35
4.17½	Oakley pass	165	3½	On		42
4.20	Worting Junc. pass	155	4	On		30
4.23	Basingstoke arr.	155	5	On	7	28
4.25½	Basingstoke dep.	185 B.O.	6	Off		40
4.33	Hook pass	175	5	On	12	42
4.35½	Winchfield pass	165	5	On	5	39
4.39	Fleet pass	180	4½	Off		43
4.42½	Farnborough pass	170	5	On	5	40
4.48	Brookwood pass	180	4½	Off		38
4.54	Woking arr.	170	5	On		35
4.57	Woking dep.	175	6	Off	8	40
5.02¼	Byfleet pass	170	5½	On		37
5.05¼	Weybridge pass	170	5½	On		39
5.07¾	Walton pass	175	5	On		40
5.10½	Esher pass	170	5	Off		36
5.14	Surbiton arr.	175	6	Off		14
5.15½	Surbiton dep.	170	6	Off	8	42
5.20¼	Malden pass	165	5½	On		40
5.21¾	Raynes Park pass	170		Off		45
5.24¼	Wimbledon pass	175	5	Off		34
5.27½	Earlsfield pass	170	5½	On		37
5.30¾	Clapham Junc. pass	175	5	Off		38
5.33¼	Queens Road pass	175		Off		
5.37¼	Vauxhall pass	165		Off		
5.42¼	Waterloo arr.	150	4½	On		

Oil used 166.6gal. or 16.9lb. per mile.

Coal used 700lb. or 8.5lb. per mile.

History might well be defined as everything that has happened a moment and more ago. The era of the Class 442 units on BR is history (some may be resurrected by the privatised railway), as is that of their electric predecessors, Reps/TCs/VEPs/BIGs/Cigs and before that CORs/PANs, etc. We might also think of transition as well, steam to electric or diesel, but how about transition from electric to electric? The late 1980s saw the end of the REP/TC workings on the Bournemouth line replaced by the 442s mentioned. In that changeover phase the traction motors from the REP units were also removed to be fitted into the new units and which resulted in a variety of combinations of TCs and EDs working the main line services. Here a pair of Class 73s power an up Waterloo service past what had previously been Lymington Junction just west of Brockenhurst. The formation is of two TC units, one of five cars having the addition of a restaurant from a withdrawn REP and the other a conventional 4TC. Such workings lasted for only a short time and it appears were rarely recorded. *Graham Smith/Richard Sissons*

The Southern Way

The regular volume for the Southern devotee

MOST RECENT BACK ISSUES

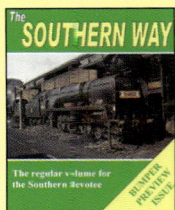

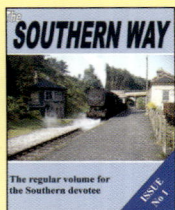

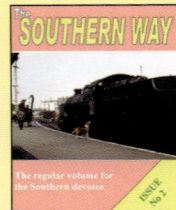

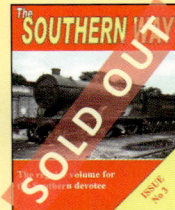

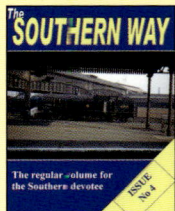

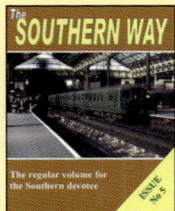

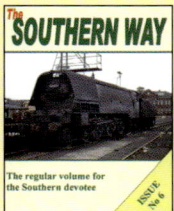

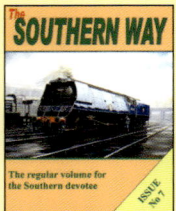

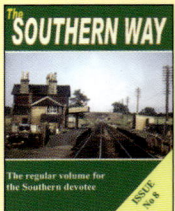

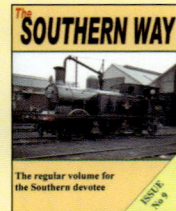

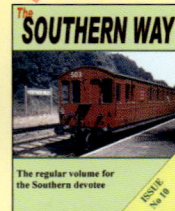

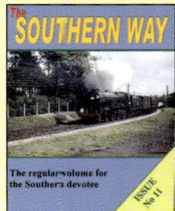

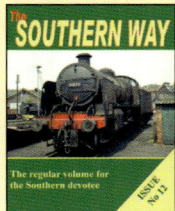

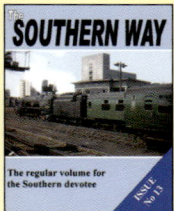

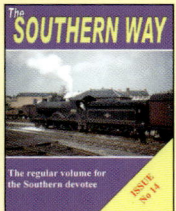

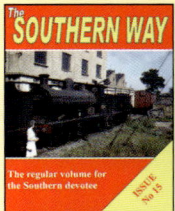

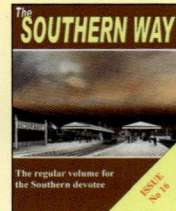

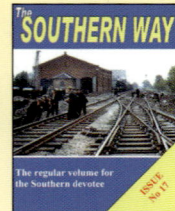

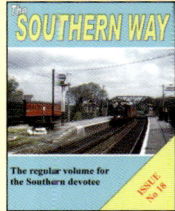

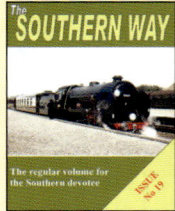

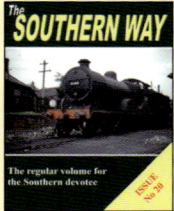

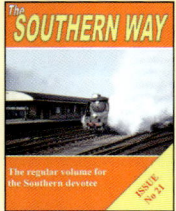

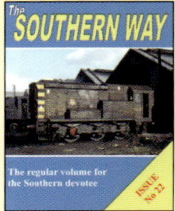

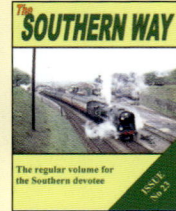

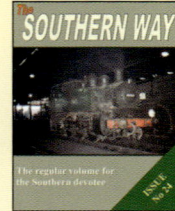

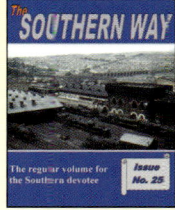

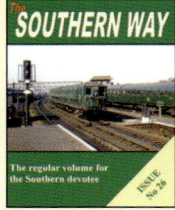

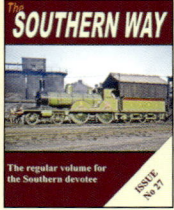

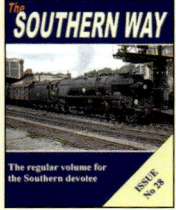

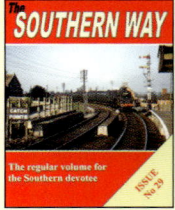

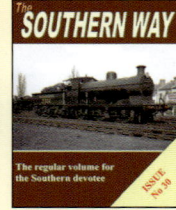

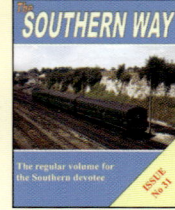

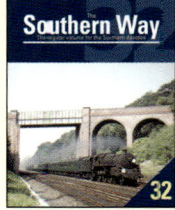

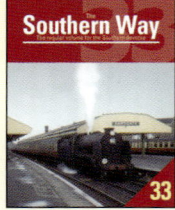

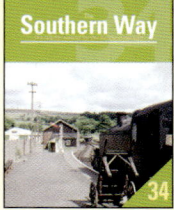

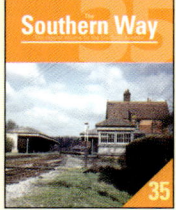

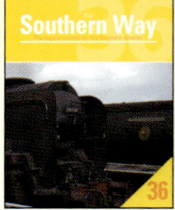

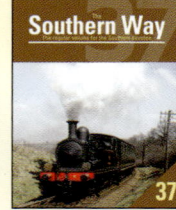

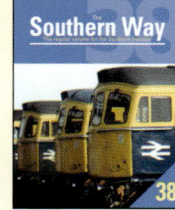

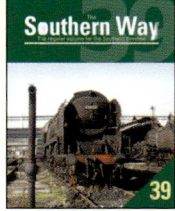

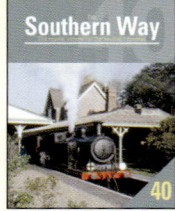

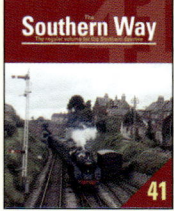

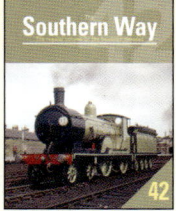

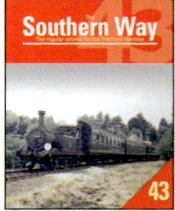

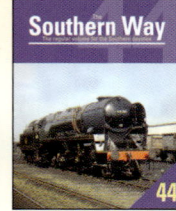

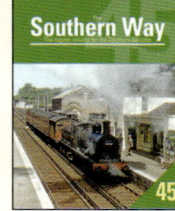

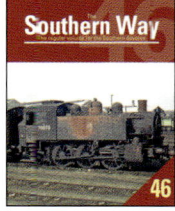

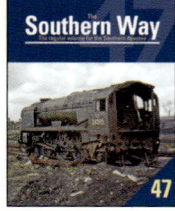

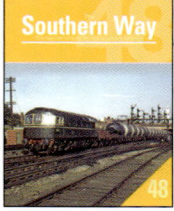

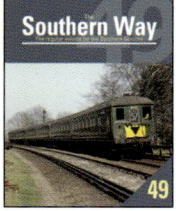

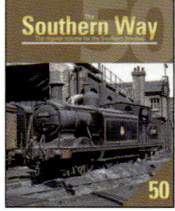

The Southern Way

The regular volume for the Southern devotee

SPECIAL ISSUES

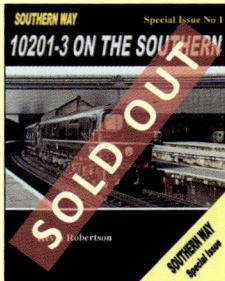

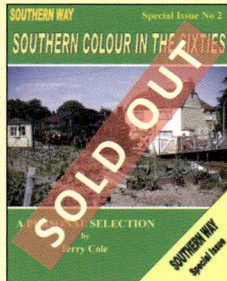

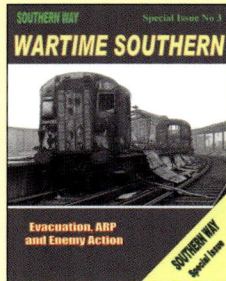

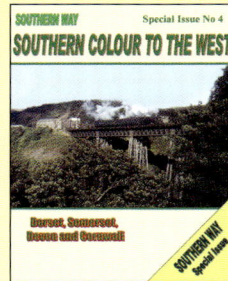

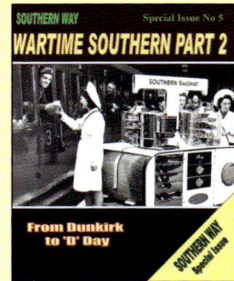

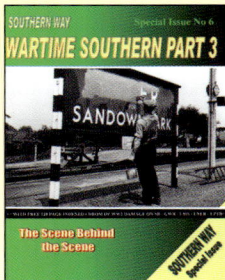

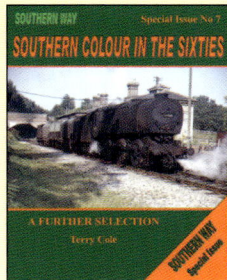

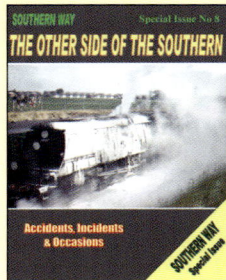

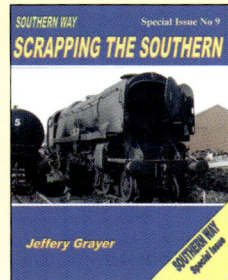

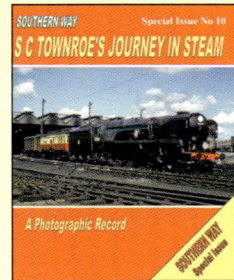

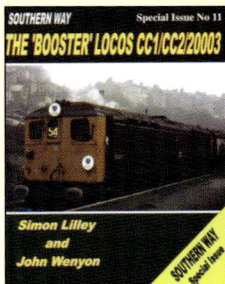

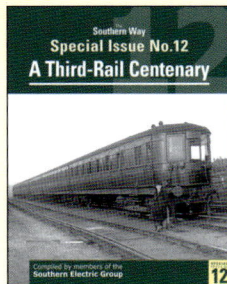

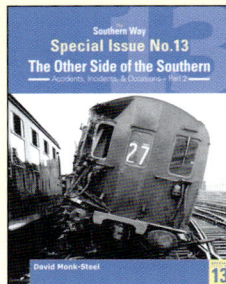

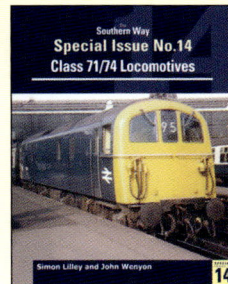

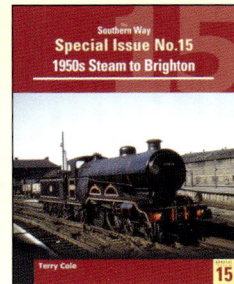

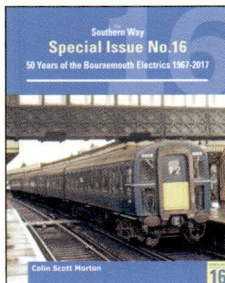

The Southern Way

The regular volume for the Southern devotee

SPECIAL ISSUE

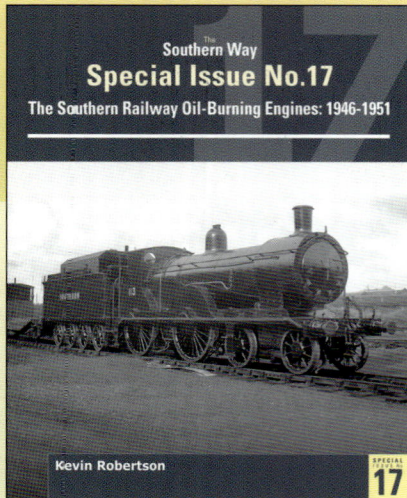

The Southern Way
Special Issue No.17
The Southern Railway Oil-Burning Engines: 1946-1951

Kevin Robertson

Southern Way Special Issue No.17 The Southern Railway Oil-Burning Engines: 1946-1951

Kevin Robertson

In 1946 the railway companies were requested by Government to explore alternatives to burning coal in order to save stocks which was desperately needed for export in order to accumulate foreign currency that could then be used to acquire other essential items in short supply.

The intention was to replace coal with oil in the fireboxes of steam locomotives. The requested timescale was totally impractical. The instruction had only been issued to the railway companies in August 1946 yet implementation was requested by January 1947. They were given a matter of months to change the way locomotives had been powered since the beginning of the railway age in the 1830s and 40s. Only two companies managed to comply in anything like the time suggested, the GWR and the Southern.

This is the story of the Southern Railway conversions, the installations required, details of the engines converted to oil burning and the duties they performed. This in-depth study of those days reveals much new information for the first time. Heavily illustrated throughout and including details of locomotive duty rosters and accounts from railwaymen involved in the episode, this is fascinating account of a short-lived but ultimately unsuccessful experiment.

96 pages, paperback

ISBN: 9781910809709 £16.95

Publication date: November 2020

Available at all good book shops, rail enthusiast shops, museums and preserved railways.

Crecy Publishing Ltd
1a Ringway Trading Est, Shadowmoss Rd, Manchester M22 5LH
Tel +44 (0)161 499 0024
www.crecy.co.uk